BRINGING MEANING INTO
MONDAY

A Sustainable Approach to Bottom Line Success

Printed in the United States of America by:

CreateSpace
100 Enterprise Way, Suite A200
Scotts Valley, CA 95066

ISBN 978-1-442-15366-0

To Mom, for everything

Table of Contents

In order to create sustainable social improvement, it must occur where people spend the majority of their time … where group relationships are conditioned.

– Confucius

Introduction

The intent of Bringing Meaning into Monday™ is to create BEST leaders, those individuals capable of achieving sustainable results by creating an empowering, productive, resilient and meaningful work climate; an environment which ...

Builds trust and accountability
Establishes shared purpose
Streamlines systems and services
Taps talent

BEST leaders establish strategic and market focus, and also reduce hierarchical bottlenecks by reengineering priorities and work practices. BEST leaders encourage their employees to think beyond self-interests and historic boundaries.

For this to occur, they must emphasize the creation of **value**; reawaken the essence of capitalism ... *achieving wealth by improving the well-being of society.* This value directly improves bottom-line performance in terms of margins, productivity and innovation, and also positively influences the workplace, families and communities.

<u>Workplace</u> effectiveness will improve as people are better equipped to answer these two questions:

- *What value results from my efforts?*
- *Is the organization stronger and more competitive due to my existence and contribution?*

1

<u>Families</u> become stronger as the positive energy produced at work, and more importantly, the skills necessary to achieve it, carryover into one's personal life.

<u>Communities</u> are the recipients of a more vibrant economy. Job opportunities will increase, new business will be attracted to the area, and civic vitality will improve as organizations and people become more inclined to contribute time, talent and treasure toward civic improvement.

Good versus BEST

This book converts good leaders into BEST leaders. Good leaders tend to motivate their followers extrinsically, managing objectives and using money, promotion and/or job security as their primary tactics. Whereas BEST leaders are able to motivate their workforce intrinsically, connecting employees' hearts with their heads and hands. Good leaders often pride themselves as decision makers. Unfortunately, over time, this strength may also be a weakness in that it often limits the degree of workforce empowerment. When faced with this leadership style, people learn to follow orders, which frequently results in compliance versus commitment. BEST leaders, while respecting decisiveness, build a work climate that is not dependent on their physical presence. They instill confidence, understanding and decision-making latitudes within their followers, empowering others to make faster and often higher-quality decisions. On the surface, this BEST approach may appear to take more time. However, once instilled, it is far more sustainable, responsive and resilient ... and yes, far more *meaningful*!

Introduction

The Complete Picture

To achieve more meaning, this book looks at two-sides of the same coin. Showing how a value-based work climate (the coin) simultaneously affects both sides. One side is the more visible, tangible side ... introducing standard, yet frequently overlooked business practices that leaders can embrace in order to simultaneously improve performance and workforce morale. The other side of the coin offers insight as to what intrinsically drives human performance. This second side is often mislabeled as "soft" and therefore is frequently underemphasized. However, for leaders to more fully embrace the value-based practices and improve their odds of implementation success, it's important they appreciate both sides.

Bringing Meaning into Monday™ provides the framework to create a value-centric, meaningful work environment. In the context of work, increased meaning is developed from a shared or higher purpose that aligns individual agendas with the organization's priorities – priorities focused on delivering value to coworkers, customers, communities, and ultimately shareholders.

Bob and Bill

You will now be introduced to **Bob and Bill**; two everyday employees in everyday jobs, dealing with everyday issues. Their dialogue will guide you through the book, providing segues between chapters and connecting concepts with reality.

Friday, 5:30 p.m. ...

 "Bob, I'm out of here. What are your plans for the weekend?" asked Bill.

"I'm hoping to take in my daughter's soccer game tomorrow morning, but I'm not sure I'll be able to," he responded.

"Why? I thought you coached her team?"

"I did, but that was before the latest changes here at work," responded Bob as he slouched even further into his chair. "Our department is swamped. More is being asked of us, yet we seem to have fewer resources available. That's why I'll probably miss tomorrow's game; I'm falling behind on a few things."

"Yeah, I know how that is," replied Bill.

"The family is not real happy with me; they're frustrated with the time I spend at work. Family dinners are becoming a thing of the past."

"Bob, you have to be careful. This place can burn you out if you let it."

"No kidding. Either we're breaking our backs to respond to increased demands or we're looking for ways to cut costs due to a market slowdown. I guess I shouldn't complain, at least I have a job."

"I agree. Feast or famine," Bill remarked. "A couple of months ago, my department was in a similar boat. We couldn't seem to keep up with demands and management wasn't willing to add bodies."

"Yeah, I've heard. Your department is getting a lot of internal press. We haven't been able to leverage the new systems the way you guys have. I'm not sure why."

"Systems? Is that the buzz going around?" asked Bill.

"Yup, that's all we've been hearing about lately," remarked Bob. "The more we question the increased workload, the more management points to using the tools and systems they've invested in. They use your department as the benchmark. The systems have helped us manage our work, but they don't help us manage unrealistic demands or declining budgets."

"Interesting," responded Bill. "If you have the time, I'd like to talk with you further about how we achieved our results. The new systems helped, but they weren't the answer."

"Is that so? I'd like to take you up on the offer. I'm just not sure when."

"I'll look forward to it," said Bill. "Now, why don't you get out of here? It's Friday!"

"I wish, but I'll be here awhile."

"Companies must enable their employees to pitch and run with new ideas – ideas that help to move us toward a sustainable world. In short, make meaning for their employees and allow them the chance to align their personal values with what they do on the job everyday."

– Stuart L. Hart, Author
Capitalism at the Crossroads

1
Why Meaning

According to separate surveys conducted by Gallup and Conference Board, nearly 50% of American workers are dissatisfied at work, actively disengaged from their job, costing the country more than $300 billion a year in lost productivity.

Quality of work life is taking on a more pronounced role in the minds of many leaders, affecting both bottom-line performance and employee morale. Gregg Easterbrook, in his book *The Progress Paradox*, echoed these views by stating "today the majority of men and women in the U.S. and European Union have acquired the living circumstances, reasonable comfort, and decent health for which previous generations yearned. Therefore, a transition from material want to meaning want is in progress on a historically unprecedented scale – involving hundreds of millions of people – and may eventually be recognized as a principle cultural development of our age." Yet, with that said, many leaders are realizing that addressing the "soft" side of human behavior is hard. Job satisfaction, to a degree, is a result of compensation and career opportunities. In large part, it is also a result of the sense of self-worth and validation the workplace provides.

In Viktor Frankl's book *Man's Search for Meaning*, he describes the hardships he personally endured within World War II concentration camps. Physical pain, starvation and death are typically not used to describe conditions found in today's workplace. Even though these conditions were inhumane and horrendous, they were not what Mr. Frankl found the most torturous. He felt the greater issue, beyond the physical extremes, was the loss of personal identity and self-worth, and the impact it had on the inner-person. He argued, "Man's main concern is not to gain pleasure or to avoid pain but rather to see a meaning in his life." Although the physical conditions found at work are not comparable to those experienced by Mr. Frankl, the issue of loss of self-identity or increased apathy is. Therefore, Mr. Frankl's solution also has relevance to work. He contends that by giving people a sense of hope in the future – a purpose for living – it will better equip them to deal in the present. By reframing a person's attitude toward difficult circumstances, they can grow from them versus succumbing to them.

More recently these sentiments are echoed by the Dalai Lama in Dr. Howard Cutler's book, *The Art of Happiness at Work*. In the words of the Dalai Lama, "If you view your work as something that is really worthwhile – if, for instance, there is a higher purpose to your work – then of course, even if the work is very hard there may be a greater willingness to undergo that hardship." He went on to say, when people "focus on the real issue, it creates greater satisfaction instead of divisions and conflicts caused when we lose sight of the wider issues and start bickering among ourselves ... your underlying motivation can change based on this wider perspective and it will build your enthusiasm to work."

Finding Me – Connecting with Others

Dr. Dean Ornish, in the *Foreword* to the book *Kitchen Table Wisdom*, stated "there is no meaning in facts." This is interesting considering his science-based medical background. He felt "our uniqueness is what gives us value and meaning ... what connects us all."

Speaking with the credibility of a medical doctor, he considered "the real epidemic in our culture is not just physical heart disease; it's what I call emotional and spiritual heart disease: the sense of loneliness, isolation, and alienation that is so prevalent in our culture because of the breakdown of the social networks that used to give us a sense of connection and community."

These observations have significant relevance within today's workplace, considering the impact work-life quality has on one's overall health. First, people are intrinsically in search of their identity, what makes them unique. And, second, people by nature require a sense of connection with others, a sense of community. This inner-need for connection, while addressed in part by family, friends and faith, is increasingly a result of the connection, or lack thereof, one attains at work. Especially considering the amount of time spent there.

Therefore, in order to stimulate a *meaningful* workplace, organizations must provide an environment that enables employees to discover their unique value and sense of contribution. In addition, people must also be able to connect their individual interests with the collective interests of the organization and/or work unit. This will result in a greater sense of community, simultaneously advancing the shared-interests of the organization and the self-interests of the individual.

While this is certainly not easy, it is achievable. Many organizations have made great strides in aligning self-interests with the shared-interests of the organization. They have developed a vision, created a strategic plan, prioritized goals, instituted common work processes, and improved communication practices; all of which helps connect individual skills and aspirations with the organization's goals and priorities. Yet, something is still missing.

While the above practices are responsible for significant performance improvement, this book will introduce another piece of the puzzle; a piece that does not diminish the importance of the aforementioned pieces, but instead augments them. This piece will bring additional Meaning into Monday by dynamically influencing daily decisions and behaviors. This, in turn, will dramatically improve cooperation, creativity and responsiveness, and result in a more engaged and connected workforce, and a more productive and resilient organization.

People and organizations are busy juggling multiple plates, pursuing the American Dream by working harder and harder versus working smarter by taking time to understand what work is still valued and what work can be eliminated. This would allow them to achieve more by doing less, focusing on the real issues, the real needs.

Therefore, in the context of work, greater meaning develops from a shared or higher purpose that aligns individual agendas with the organization's priorities – priorities focused on delivering value to others. The remainder of this book will address how this is achieved.

Friday, 5:30 p.m. … continuing dialogue

"Bob, I wanted to mention something else." interjected Bill.

"What's that?" replied Bob, giving Bill a rather quizzical look.

"What has occurred here at work has had an equally profound effect on me personally, outside work."

"In what way?" asked Bob, curious as to where the conversation was heading.

"It's clear to me that my relationship with my wife and children has improved significantly. I'm more aware of their needs."

"In terms of 'quality time'?" asked Bob.

"Actually, beyond that. Yes, I've been able to spend more time with them; however, it goes a bit deeper than that."

"How so?"

"You know how we face a great deal of pressure here at work? And, how the changes within my department have helped us better deal with increasing demands, even difficult relationships?" Bill continued.

"Yeah, I guess, although I must say that you have a more positive outlook than I do."

"Well, it's clear to me that my family is facing similar pressures, albeit different ones. Our lives continue to accelerate, throwing us a variety of curves. Can you relate?" asked Bill.

"No kidding. I certainly see the strains that school and peer pressures have on my children. Often it's rather dramatic, and I'm not sure I can fully relate with them," remarked Bob. "It seems that due to cell phones, Facebook and the Internet, they are faced with different challenges than what we faced years ago."

"I agree," responded Bill. "And that's my point. Stress isn't just a workplace phenomenon, it's all around us. I don't know this for sure, but I believe our children, in particular, are struggling to keep up."

"I couldn't agree more," replied Bob, realizing that he often feels ill-equipped to provide parental guidance.

"Well, what I wanted to say is that I've been able to re-apply some of what I'm learning here at work within my family. It seems, although I'm not entirely sure how, that the changes in my department have given me new outlooks and skills," offered Bill.

"Such as?" inquired Bob.

"Previously, I tended to negatively react to my kids problems, often leading to arguments. Suffice to say, I wasn't being too helpful. However, now I'm better able to help them assess particular situations, proactively helping them consider alternative responses. Now, it appears that they value my help, even seek me out. It has certainly improved our relationships."

"Bill, that's very interesting. I'm glad you shared it. I can relate with what you're saying. I've often wondered if I'm making a positive difference in my kids' lives."

"Individual commitment to a group effort - that is what makes a team work, a company work, a society work, a civilization work."

– Vince Lombardi

2
Why Work

The workplace offers fertile ground for personal and societal improvement. Positive energy generated at work will carryover into society, making families and communities stronger. It's logical; the more people are valued and the more they experience the positive effects of encouragement, teamwork, support and even love, the more apt they are to extend it to others. As people learn to respect diversity, reconcile differences, and frankly get along with people unlike themselves, the world in and outside of work will dramatically improve.

Much like food provides nourishment to the body, a meaningful, collaborative and value-based work atmosphere provides the fuel or nourishment to an organization. It is common sense; however, achieving common sense has unfortunately proven not so common.

The more self-interests and/or individual agendas are aligned with a higher purpose and serving others, the more the quality of the social atmosphere and the degree of cooperation will correspondingly improve. People are social creatures, not machines. They will extract more meaning and purpose from their jobs the more the social atmosphere and the quality of relationships improve. Their creativity and productivity will improve, as will their energy levels, motivation and commitment to their jobs.

---

*The mind operates in the context of attitudes and emotions
that are conditioned by the individual's group relationships.
Unless experiences in this latter area dispose one to cooperate,
reason is likely to do nothing but aid self-interest.*

- Confucius

Confucius believed that in order to create sustainable social improvement it is "conditioned by the individual's group relationships" and, therefore, must occur where people spend the majority of their time. Today, unlike in Confucius's era, people spend the majority of their time at work away from their families, friends and faith. Therefore, the quality of the group relationships found at work, and the degree they emphasize cooperation, will significantly determine a person's overall outlook toward life.

When communities or institutions become fractured, where individual agendas outweigh the importance of the greater good, they welcome a more collaborative and shared approach. Rallying cultures, nations, communities or organizations around a common flag or shared purpose is age-old. Confucius solved tribal conflicts in China by offering a social structure that accommodated the shared interests of previously warring tribes. America was founded on shared ideals. Capitalism flourished due to the focus on providing societal value. And virtually all religions originated in order to provide a sense of shared purpose and a social structure that banded together previously fractured societies or viewpoints.

Today, however, the workplace plays a more pronounced role in influencing sustainable social improvement. *Work conditions group relationships* either positively or negatively. Focusing

16

employees and work units on the value they provide to others will align splintered agendas, and in terms of productivity and profitability, directly improve bottom-line performance. This will address the immediate needs of today's leaders and simultaneously provide employees with a unifying sense of shared purpose, aligning their self-interests with a common cause.

For purposes here, we must keep in mind that generating value, improving margins, and creating an engaged and productive workforce are outcomes; outcomes that *all* organizations desire. Yet *how* it is achieved will also condition relationships, behaviors, attitudes and mindsets that, when carried outside of work, will result in healthier families and communities.

When organizations, for bottom-line reasons, *intentionally* reorient the workplace toward a more value-based environment, they will discover the need to simultaneously transform individual mindsets and historical biases. In today's increasingly complex and diverse world, individuals will be required to look *inward* in order to improve their *outward* ability to work effectively with different people, different beliefs, different worldviews and different situations. People, in order to remain relevant and employed, will need to gain comfort addressing their inner-world, their inner-beliefs. While training can help generalize concepts and possibly surface blind spots, this is a personal quest, a pursuit of inner-discovery, inner-growth.

This journey will not just affect the employee, improving their productivity, creativity, resilience and health, but it will also impact the person by simultaneously addressing all aspects of their life outside of work. For example, their roles as parent, spouse, sibling, friend, coach and volunteer are all areas where they have the ability to positively influence others. However, this assumes that a) they have personally experienced the positive effects of inner-transformation; and b) that they have attained methods and skills that can be reapplied outside of work – they have become conscious and competent.

Whack-a-Mole

A multitude of problems face today's families and communities. For example, violence affects both families and communities, as does various forms of addiction, abuse or bullying, divorce, unprotected sex and obesity. It doesn't stop there. Our educational system, more specifically the ability for children to learn, is weakening. The healthcare system is broken, as is individual accountability for personal health. I could go on, but the point is we have many societal problems. A lot of time, money and resources are being directed at solving these and many other social problems, yet, if we are honest with ourselves they have been met with marginal success. Entitlement programs haven't worked, nor is there enough money in the pipeline to sustain them.

It seems the manner in which we're addressing many of today's societal problems can be compared to a popular children's arcade game, *Whack-a-Mole*. In this game, the player uses a large mallet to whack the head of a mole as it surfaces above the table only to discover additional mole heads popping up that need to be whacked. Unfortunately, this game is being played out in many families, organizations and communities, continually shifting attention from one mole head to another. Billions of tax dollars are being spent attempting to smash mole heads into submission, only to discover that the game seemingly never ends. Interestingly, players skilled at playing this game are rewarded, yet, truth be told, our social engine is stuck in reverse.

Success needs to be redefined. Whacking mole heads has all the appearances of progress, irrespective of the fact that many of the moles previously whacked continue to resurface. People and/or social initiatives should not be judged simply on their ability to whack moles, but also on their ability to prevent them from resurfacing. BEST leaders attack the game from a different angle; they address the underlying or intrinsic factors that reside beneath the table, and, as a result, they create more sustainable relationships, stronger families, and healthier organizations and communities.

These underlying or inner-skills can and, for bottom-line reasons, must be learned at work. Organizations can no longer succeed in isolation, protecting historic practices and/or self-interests. This makes them incapable of effectively leveraging resources and/or fully tapping the diverse talents of people both within and outside their organizations.

Fortunately, skills learned at work and mindsets conditioned at work will not stay at work.

It Takes a Village

For all the right reasons, generations of Americans have focused on improving the standard of living and quality of life for future generations. In large part, they have succeeded, but this prosperity comes with a price. People are expending a great deal of energy attempting to keep up with the Jones'. They are working longer and harder in order to advance a standard of living that previous generations couldn't even imagine possible. The problem is, while one hand seeks to maximize our generation's standard of living, we need to keep in mind that the other hand is still responsible to rock the cradle of the next generation.

In their book, *Ghosts from the Nursery*, authors Robin Karr-Morse and Meredith S. Wiley stated, "America has valued self-reliance, independence, and toughness … [yet] these ideals without balance may actually be our undoing. It appears that while we have put great effort toward protecting ourselves from external dangers, the greatest threat is from internal deterioration of the soft tissue at our nation's core."

Throughout the early 1900s people moved from the farms into the cities in order to find better paying jobs and materially improve their standard of living. It worked. Organizations were able to pool people together, pay them fairly, and mass-produce products in order to feed continually increasing consumer demands. As a result, a large part of an individual's identity and sense of community is found within the organization versus what previously was the community or family they were a part of. Traditionally organizations have valued employees for their talents and contribution, and, in return, employees valued the paycheck. Employer-employee relationships were more transactional in nature, not communal. As a result over time, people have lost the sense of an extended community; they left the village behind.

Leadership practices taught during much of the twentieth century were consistent with what industries required; mass production, marketing, sales and distribution, with very little emphasis in providing workers with motivation, meaning and fulfillment. Industry believed people were largely motivated by the almighty dollar – a good days pay for a good days work. However, social signals, albeit silent ones have begun to surface. Aging baby-boomers have reached a level of material prosperity not imagined by the generation that preceded them, and subsequent generations have their physiological, security and monetary needs largely met. As a result, employees are looking for more than compensation and safe working conditions; they are seeking opportunities to increase their intrinsic worth and self actualization. Everybody seeks fair pay and opportunities for career advancement; however, people want to intrinsically know their efforts are valued by others. Much of their individual identity will result from an increased sense of teamwork, community, purpose and contribution to the greater good; which, in the context of work, develops from a shared or higher purpose that aligns individual agendas with the organization's priorities – priorities focused on delivering value to others.

Friday, 5:35 p.m. ...

"Bill, before you go, can I ask you something?" asked Bob, appearing a bit uncomfortable.

"What's up?"

"Lately, I seem to be running on empty. I'm working long hours and it's taking a toll on me both physically and emotionally. Maybe it's a rhetorical question, but I've been wondering just how much of my pressures at work impact my life away from work."

"I can relate with what you're saying," replied Bill. "A few months ago I was in a similar state. I was worn out. At the time, I believed all the off-hour demands were the culprit. I've since realized I was bringing work home with me – not literally, but emotionally."

"What did you do?" asked Bob, realizing Bill was addressing exactly what he was feeling.

"Not much," admitted Bill. "I believed it was normal."

"I'm not sure I follow you. What changed? You seem to be a different person; I've never seen you as happy as you've been the last couple of months."

"As it turned out I wasn't the only one experiencing these issues," responded Bill. "Our department was experiencing high absenteeism, quality issues and a spike in customer complaints. I believe this is why our department decided to change the way we managed our work. I must say I'm grateful. It's improved my productivity and energy here at work, but also has had a positive effect on my personal life."

"Bill, I know you have to go, but you've given me a valuable insight. I've been reluctant to discuss this issue with anybody because I believed it was something I needed to address. You've helped me realize the issue is a bit deeper than I thought. I'm going to check with a few others and compare notes."

"Good luck Bob. I'm glad I could help. I look forward to hearing about what you discover."

"It's the action, not the fruit of the action, that's important. You have to do the right thing. It may not be in your power, may not be in your time, that there'll be any fruit. But that doesn't mean you stop doing the right thing. You may never know what results come from your action. But if you do nothing, there will be no result."

– Mahatma Gandhi

3
Why Now

*"Neither you nor the world knows what you can do
until you have tried."*

– Ralph Waldo Emerson

Many employees are physically and mentally depleted when they leave work. The effects of dysfunctional work relationships leave people emotionally drained, and people who lack a strong sense of purpose are virtually untapped spiritually. As a result many people are frustrated, exhausted, unhappy and unfilled, which means they are less likely to be active in social stewardship and more likely to be out of step with the needs of their family.

The workplace is well-positioned to influence positive societal change – out of necessity – not choice. Organizations are living communities. Energy, attitudes and skills produced at work (positive or negative) do not stay there. They carry over into our personal lives directly influencing our personal sense of identity and happiness; relationships with family and others; and our involvement in volunteerism and charitable giving. To be a positive influence, organizations must integrate universal principles like acceptance, respect, empathy, encouragement and cooperation deeper into the workplace – not just for altruistic purposes, but for bottom line ones as well.

In today's interconnected and dynamic marketplace, organizations require a more adaptive and resilient workforce. They require people skilled at reconciling differences, dealing with variation and finding creative solutions buried amongst diverse viewpoints. Sustainable success is no longer the result of inbreeding, but of welcoming relationships with people who share dissimilar – even opposing – worldviews, beliefs and practices.

In order to fully exploit future economic opportunities, institutions must establish cooperative networks in order to deal with the realities of today's high-risk, high-speed society. Consequently, successful companies have to continually transform themselves – shifting provincial thinking toward more integrative and co-creative thinking.

A Changing World

The world is becoming smaller and more interconnected, increasing the pace and complexity of life. Everyone needs to develop the agility, skills and resiliency to deal with this pace. Where better for this to occur than where many people spend the majority of their time – at work.

The global marketplace, information technology, and advances in communication and transportation will continue to reshape the business landscape. In addition to affecting organizations doing business in multiple geographies, globalization directly affects local businesses as their products, services and even resources become globally available. Leaders, therefore, are being challenged to revisit hierarchical and historic practices and beliefs, seeking ways to speed decision making and increase empowerment in order to respond to an accelerating marketplace. Often the beliefs and practices originally established to advance and protect local self-interests are the same ones that stand in the way of adapting to a more interconnected economy.

Successful organizations continually transform themselves in response to evolving marketplace realities. They reorient their local beliefs in order to better align with today's flatter and faster world, encouraging their employees to think beyond self interests and historic boundaries. Success is no longer a result of self-sufficiency, but more of increased interdependence. This interdependence makes it easier to leverage the resources and knowledge required to optimize time, costs and risks associated with creating and delivering value to others. As Thomas Freidman suggests in *The World Is Flat: A Brief History of the Twenty-First Century*, a flatter world necessitates a more collaborative response. Short- and long-term results will improve as organizations find new ways to leverage global knowledge and resources by drawing upon a continual influx of talented people capable of achieving balance between their individual agendas and the priorities and shared interests of the greater good.

In this global, fast-paced marketplace, customers no longer tolerate a decision-making cycle that takes days, weeks or months. The quality of response is now judged in minutes and seconds. Today's BEST leaders, in turn, rely less on their positional power and more on their ability to align, motivate and empower their employees. To achieve this, BEST leaders reduce handoffs and internal obstacles by establishing a sense of shared purpose, which improves relationship quality and broadens decision-making latitudes. As a result, this builds trust and accountability and better taps talent both within and outside the organization. BEST leaders streamline systems and services, replacing low-value activities and antiquated work practices in order to deliver high-value results. With that in mind, increased value may be generated by doing less – a rather profound, yet timely thought.

Throughout Mr. Freidman's book, he conveys a rather compelling picture of today's global reality. From numerous angles, he shows how advances in market democracy, information technology and telecommunications, and outsourcing, insourcing and offshoring continue to shrink the world.

Previously untapped synergies are surfacing due to both improved information access and the ability to share knowledge and resources. Foreign countries (e.g., India) are now in America's backyard due to the fiber optic infrastructure laid in the early 2000s. Organizations who previously had to hire skilled people in order to ensure access to them are now finding it increasingly more convenient and cost effective to access various competencies by tapping into the global knowledge bank and resource pools.

Many Americans are already experiencing the effects of global outsourcing; however, this outsourcing currently affects manufacturing and information services jobs. As idea creation and product design slowly shift offshore, there will be even more significant consequences to the American economy.

Mr. Freidman cites how twenty years ago Americans would have never imagined their global dominance in basketball, as measured every four years in the Olympics, would evaporate like it has. He uses this as an example of how the U.S. fell asleep at the wheel; the rest of the world has caught up, even in some respects surpassed the United States. Friedman cites similar declines in the manufacturing sector and the quality of education. As science and engineering leadership continues to shift offshore so, he claims, will the quality of life Americans have come to enjoy.

While he does not address it directly, another reason for the decline of U.S. basketball dominance could be the focus and mentality of many U.S. players. The game, due to TV dollars, endorsements and free agent contracts, has become, to a large degree, everybody looking out for himself. While American players focused on refining their *individual* skills, skills and statistics that make them personally more marketable, the rest of the world focused on the game of basketball, how to play as a *team.*

Driving the Point Home

The U.S. auto industry is struggling to compete with Asian automotive companies. In some respects, their inability to compete is based on quality and cost; but more importantly, it is a result of the quality of relationships with employees, suppliers, dealers and end-consumers. Rather than staying in touch with the evolving needs of their markets, customers and employees, U.S. auto companies became more inward focused, protecting turf, creating silos and losing touch with the emotive realities of business. Unfortunately, they embraced a more transactional approach to these relationships, focusing primarily on their short-term self-interests and bottom line.

When U.S. auto companies had a captive audience, they benefited economically from this transactional approach; however, in the process they slowly eroded relationship trust and constrained the long-term viability of many of their so-called partners and employees. In contrast, Asian companies continue to place high value on the quality, intimacy, heritage and interdependent nature of these same relationships.

Rather than openly recognizing this issue, U.S. auto companies believe their Asian competitors have an unfair, even cultural, advantage. Yes, in this case the Asians do have an advantage, but it is not necessarily a cultural one; it is a common sense one. They have not lost sight of the value and heritage of relationships, nor do they take them lightly or treat them in a short-term transactional or disposable manner. American companies are quickly discovering that Asian companies have significant cost, quality and supply advantages due to the strength of these historic and now global relationships. Yet, rather than stepping up to the relationship quality issues they have, U.S. automotive companies instead seek political and economic restrictions. They are searching for short-term answers to compensate for long-term negligence.

There were earlier signs of relationship erosion, yet, to a large degree, they were ignored. Studies are continually showing signs of declining employee morale and customer loyalty, and labor uprisings are becoming a daily front-page occurrence. As stated earlier, recent Gallup surveys and Conference Board studies have shown a decline in workplace satisfaction; employees are becoming increasingly more disengaged from their jobs.

As the U.S. auto industry example shows, this house-of-cards leadership style is beginning to backfire and is being exploited by savvy global competitors. Asian companies, in this example, do have a distinct advantage. It should serve as a wake-up call to the U.S. auto industry and possibly business practices in general.

It is time to reassemble Humpty Dumpty. A rebalancing must occur and increased attention must be paid to serving others and the quality of relationships within and outside of today's organizations. People do not need to sacrifice their individualistic or material ideals; instead, they must rediscover that a shared and interdependent approach is a better route to achieve them.

Reawakening the Dream

"The fall of the American Dream may be inevitable. We Americans may find ourselves like the proverbial 'odd man out,' grossly out of step with the changes taking place all around us as the human race enters a global era."

– Jeremy Rifkin, Author
The European Dream

Few people would deny the material prosperity found in the American dream, yet, for purposes here, it is important to also recognize the societal costs. Since 1960 the average disposable income in America increased more than two-fold (taking inflation into account). At the same time depression has increased anywhere between three to ten times. Violent crime rates have increased four times. The prison population has escalated five times. The divorced population increased seven times. Teen suicides have increased three times, and the percentage of babies to unwed mothers has increased six-fold. Statistics such as these suggest not all is well; unfortunately there's more.

According to a 2005 report titled *State of America's Children*, published by the Children's Defense Fund, each day in America 2,482 children are confirmed as abused or neglected, 4,356 are arrested, and 16,964 public school students are suspended. America, when compared to twenty-five other industrialized countries, ranks first in GDP, defense expenditures, and the number of millionaires and billionaires. Yet the country ranks dead last in protecting children against gun violence, twenty-third in infant mortality, and eighteenth in the percent of children living in poverty.

While children may have parents, many lack a quality relationship with their mom and dad. As a result many children are turning to peers, television, media, and sports and entertainment figures to define their worldview and moral character. This is unfortunate and unsustainable.

Today's institutions, business and civic, must assume some accountability for both the problem and, more importantly, the solution. Progress cannot necessarily be slowed; yet a different approach is required. While family, friends and faith influence our overall quality of life, work, given the amount of time spent there, has an even more profound effect.

Like it or not, technology advances and globalization are radically changing the face of business. Today's organizations must transform themselves in response to evolving market and workplace realities, reengineering their local beliefs and practices in order to better align with today's flatter and faster world. Success does not result from doing everything; it results from doing the right things.

Work, by its very nature, provides a fertile environment in which to individually grow. Not, however, via increased comfort or reduced work load, but instead by developing one's ability to cope with the chaos and tension that naturally results from an accelerating business climate. By allowing daily events to penetrate deeper into their inner-psyche, and by virtue of human's reflective and adaptive faculties, people will grow and evolve. Self-awareness increases, which in turn increases relationship quality, energy levels and their personal resilience in coping with the turbulence of everyday life. Where better for this to occur than where many people spend the majority of their time – at work.

Today's leaders are the hinge upon which the door swings. They are accountable for establishing a shared vision, and more importantly, building the workforce commitment necessary to pursue it. Leaders capable of tapping into the intrinsic need that individuals have for a greater sense of purpose will find an infinite and perpetual source of motivation far less costly to administer and ultimately far more sustainable.

While leaders may intellectually agree with the growing importance of relationship quality, sense of purpose and contributing value to others, the fact is they are byproducts of a material world, wherein logic, facts and bottom-line results rule the day. They respect the inherent value of humanistic traits such as mutual respect, listening, empathy, encouragement and the value of serving others; however, they often find it difficult to connect them directly to the bottom line. As a result, these traits are classified as 'soft,' and frequently underemphasized. Respecting this reality, we must go beyond encouraging a "kinder, gentler place to work" and show how teamwork, co-creation, constructive confrontation and the desire to create value positively affects the organization's short- and long-term viability. In addition, these traits must be reinforced via social structures (e.g., strategies, work practices and measures) that condition and nurture group relationships. In this case, those relationships found at work.

To be effective in today's interconnected and dynamic era, leaders must embrace their softer side; yet for hard, bottom-line reasons. They require self-awareness, reflective faculties, imagination, agility and a sense of purpose in order to fully engage their employees. In addition, elements that are important in one organization or situation may not be equally relevant in another; therefore today's leaders must be transformative versus transactional, skilled at managing change and building workforce commitment, capable of reflecting reality not necessarily idealism.

In addition to establishing vision, strategies, core values and objectives, effective leaders must also align their people closer to the ever-changing, more operational voice of their external and internal clients – the recipients of their products and services. BEST leaders must continually streamline systems and services, rewarding employees based on their individual and collective ability to capture, aggregate, analyze and react to the dynamic needs and priorities of those they serve. This will achieve more material results while simultaneously instilling greater social responsibility, cooperation, creativity and sense of service – intrinsic traits – within the workforce. Bottom-line performance will improve, in terms of profitability, growth and innovation, and due to this value-oriented approach, employees' will extract more meaning and fulfillment from their jobs. This results in higher quality relationships and a more sustainable, healthy and productive work climate.

In a nutshell, today's organizations and today's leaders play an instrumental role in reawakening the American Dream – economic and social.

Wednesday 8:30 a.m. ...

 "Bill, after our discussion last Friday, I spoke with a few other people, including our team leader and department manager. There was some initial reluctance as they believe our department has different issues than yours, but everybody was willing to talk."

"And?" replied Bill.

"They are all feeling the strain and overload, and they were all receptive to ANYTHING that could help ease the pressures and improve the work climate."

"We're talking about some pretty significant stuff here," Bill said. "Simply improving the work climate was not enough to motivate people to change. You would think it was, but it wasn't."

"It's interesting you say that," replied Bob. "Although I didn't expect it, my discussions with others seemed to surface a number of other challenges we're facing. Many of them are affecting our competitiveness."

"For example?" asked Bill.

"I'm not sure where to start; most of the comments revolved around the changing world. Many people initially believed that globalization only affects multi-national companies, but it became clear that it is also affecting organizations like ours."

"Any specifics?"

"Lots. One obvious one is the Internet. A few years ago, the Internet was the domain of computer geeks. Now people are turning to it for all sorts of information. We have Google to thank for that!"

"How has that affected your department?"

"Are you kidding? Speed for one thing, information access another. Previously we held the cards, now answers are available on the Net. There's a wealth of global knowledge out there … it's changing how the game is played."

"Interesting. Anything else?"

"Outsourcing!"

"Touchy subject."

"People, including myself, are real emotional about this. Loss of jobs and the continual increase of imports are responsible for driving down U.S. prices and wages. It's easy to get angry."

"What's the upside?"

"Well, we began to realize that if the lower-value work could be shifted to places that can do it better, faster and cheaper, it would free our time up to do more creative, value-added and rewarding work. In a manner of speaking, we control our own destiny."

"I'm impressed Bob."

"Bill, people have begun to really open up with me. They are frustrated with their jobs; many people are simply going through the motions. They do what's asked but that's about it."

"I'm not surprised. Unfortunately, people have fallen into the trap of believing work can't be fun."

"Exactly," replied Bob. "I just wish management understood this. They don't seem to care about the people.

"I felt the same way, but not any longer."

"What do you mean?" blurted Bob. "I thought that was what we've been discussing all along."

"Well, from *our* perspective that is exactly what we've been discussing. However, if you look at this issue from management's perspective, there is more to it."

"What is more important than having happy employees?"

"I would have agreed, before we went through the last few months," replied Bill. "I, like you, believed that it was management's responsibility to make the employees happy and satisfied, and for years they've tried. We're paid well. They improved our benefit plans, established career ladders, improved communication, and even took time to celebrate progress. While their efforts help, the stress and frustration remained."

"Bill, where are you going? If you're now going to tell me that pay or promotion isn't important, you're losing me."

"That's not what I'm saying. It's just that pay and promotion are not enough. Would you agree?" Bob nodded his assent. "Management spends a lot of time implementing efforts directed toward satisfying us, but it would actually make more sense for management to focus on improving the quality and effectiveness of our work environment. We're willing to work hard if we can see the impact our efforts are having on fellow coworkers, or better yet, our end-customers. But that too seems difficult. As a result, many people have tuned out."

"Groups that develop a shared consciousness can perform tasks fluidly, efficiently, cooperatively and in coordination, with minimal communication. An intuitive connection or empathy gives people the ability to anticipate the actions, thoughts, or words of others in the group; as a result, teammates work as a unit rather than as an aggregate of individuals."

– Duane Elgin, Author
Promise Ahead

4

Achieving Balance

Take a minute and answer the following questions; use a 1-5 scale to rank the importance of each one to you. Total each column.

	Importance
	Low **1 – 5** High
1. Compensation (pay, benefits and office aesthetics & resources)	___
2. Relationship Quality, Sense of Camaraderie and Teamwork	___
3. Career Opportunity or Advancement	___
4. Sense of Purpose or the Ability to Make a Difference	___
5. Knowledge, Status, Influence or Power	___
6. Ability to Positively Impact Others (customers and/or colleagues)	___
Totals:	

There are no right answers. Depending on your current situation and/or stage in life, your answers would likely change. The point is *all* six elements play an important role in one's work life. They *all* play a role in determining the degree of engagement, meaning and happiness individuals will extract from their job.

Like a teeter-totter, life requires weight on both sides in order to make the ride meaningful. Material interests (e.g., compensation, career opportunities and status) represent side A, the odd numbered questions above. Relationship quality, sense of purpose and contributing value to the lives of *others* represents side B, the even numbered questions. Side A is more extrinsic, side B is more intrinsic. Your column totals reflect the importance or weight you put on each side.

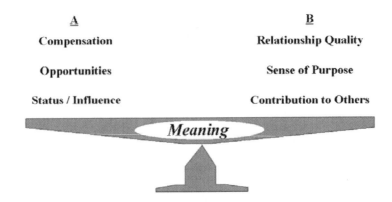

Many organizations have become over-reliant on compensation and benefit programs (side A) to motivate their employees; in the process they may be overlooking or under developing side B. As a result, these organizations fail to fully engage their workforce, head *and* heart, though they frequently spend a lot of money trying.

Therefore, increased meaning can be achieved by adding weight to side B. In the context of work, this is achieved by establishing a shared purpose that aligns individual agendas with the organization's priorities – priorities that are focused on delivering value to others. While individuals, via their interpersonal skills and ability to deal with variation, play a role in realizing a meaningful and productive environment, the organization plays an equal, if not a more important role.

Organizations must structurally enable a cohesive and meaningful workplace, an environment that is strategically unified, and one that emphasizes service to others and value creation. By structurally aligning individual agendas and work practices with organizational priorities focused on delivering value to others, successful organizations will add weight to side B. This will intrinsically improve morale, while continuing to address the extrinsic or material needs of side A, improving productivity, innovation and economic performance.

A Healthy Culture

Stress, a precursor to chronic conditions such as hypertension, obesity and depression, accounts for 60-90% of doctor visits and, to a degree, is a symptom of a larger societal problem – workplace discontent. This larger problem, in addition to impacting healthcare costs, simultaneously affects productivity, creativity and absenteeism, all bottom-line challenges facing many of today's employers.

Realizing this, employers are beginning to acknowledge the importance of work-life quality. Creating a sense of community, shared responsibility and ownership of corporate success are elements associated with a healthy lifestyle – an emotional connection with others – and have a measurable effect on the viability of organizational success.

The National Institute of Occupational Safety (NIOSH) in January 2005 published a report entitled "Examining the Value of Integrating Occupational Health and Safety and Health Promotion Programs in the Workplace." They define a healthy culture as an organization that clearly articulates the importance of individual contributions to organizational success, and the value of human capital in achieving organizational goals. An organization possessing these values will be most successful in putting in place an integrated model of health, safety and productivity management.

Unfortunately, many of today's organizations tend to be hierarchical, even bureaucratic. Inconsistent planning processes and/or historic work practices are frequently out of sync with daily realities. Conflicting or misinterpreted agendas negatively impact work-life quality, which, in turn, yields a compliant workforce versus an empowered and impassioned one. As a result, the relationship and emotional stress caused at work directly affects a person's overall health and quality of life inside and outside of work. In response, many organizations have attempted to offset deteriorating health and rising healthcare costs by introducing wellness programs that encourage healthier lifestyles. While these programs address part of the issue, Dr. Dee Edington, a foremost advocate for workforce health from the University of Michigan, suggests there is more. In a 2008 WELCOA expert interview entitled *Culture Counts ... A New Approach to Changing Unhealthy Behaviors*, he stated "by pushing behavior change without having a supportive culture in place, we've pointed a lot of people down the road that ultimately leads to failure."

In this context, failure relates to the individuals' inability or unwillingness to assume personal accountability for their health. And failure also applies at the organizational level when you consider rising healthcare costs and, more importantly, the negative affect declining workforce health has on productivity, creativity and teamwork. It appears the current *Whack-a-Mole* approach is not working. Quite possibly, it's because many well-intentioned health advocates have failed to recognize the importance of a supportive culture, instead being too fixated on pushing a particular program or solution – whacking at mole-heads versus attacking the root causes. Or, what seems to be occurring recently, a 'supportive culture' is narrowly defined as one that reinforces or incentivizes individual behavior change (e.g., weight loss, stop smoking, joining health clubs). If the definition of wellness was expanded beyond physical health, and included emotional, social and spiritual health, it would also expand the definition of a supportive or healthy culture and in turn the approaches taken to improve it.

By revisiting the conclusions of the NIOSH study, it seems they had this expanded view in mind when they defined *a healthy culture is an organization that clearly articulates the importance of individual contributions to organizational success, and the value of human capital in achieving organizational goals.* In order to enable a supportive, productive and healthy workplace, organizational leaders must structurally align individual agendas and work practices around the ever-changing needs and priorities of those they serve (i.e., their customers and coworkers). While improving productivity, creativity and relationship quality, a work culture that emphasizes value creation and delivery will also result in a greater sense of unity and shared purpose – in a word, engagement. Employees will have greater visibility as to how they individually and collectively contribute value to the lives of others, which in turn, provides them the intrinsic motivation – emotional, social and spiritual – to maintain the quality of theirs.

In essence, as the earlier teeter-totter graphically depicted, NIOSH is recommending that organizations add weight to side B, the intrinsic side, which in large part can be achieved by emphasizing value creation.

Picking up where their conversation left off ...

"Bill, you make a good point. When I think about it, what I'm paid is fair, although I wouldn't admit it," offered Bob. "What really frustrates me is we seem to have lost the spark in our department. People are cynical, and teamwork has really suffered. People are reluctant to share ideas or make improvement suggestions."

"I can relate," remarked Bill. "Personally, before our department changed, I was in the same boat. It seemed to me that people were just out for themselves. We weren't unified, and that led to numerous conflicts."

"What did you do about it?"

"It was clear everyone had different interpretations of what was being asked of them. Management worked hard to keep us informed, but it got to the point where we had to have daily meetings in order to reconcile our differences. It became clear our monthly planning process was broken. Things were changing so fast, we needed to get our arms around it."

"Really? How?"

"A few months ago we started to better manage expectations. Our department, like yours, was really lean on resources and budgets didn't allow us to add people. Demands continued to increase. We were going nuts; lots of stress, confusion and bickering. By better managing expectations, or service levels, we have improved the situation dramatically."

"In what way," asked Bob.

"Basically, we are better equipped to say yes *and* no," replied Bill.

44

"I'm having a problem following you. I can understand how it helps your department, but saying 'no' must frustrate those others you support."

"Not at all. There was some initial confusion, but we have dramatically improved both our productivity and client satisfaction levels. Initially, you thought it was because of the IT systems we put in place. They helped, but they were not the answer."

"Wait a minute; stop right there. Now you are really confusing me. Didn't you say earlier that your department is saying 'no' to some of their demands? But now you just said your productivity and satisfaction has gone up. I'm struggling to see how," responded Bob.

"We all felt the same early on. It didn't make sense and a lot of us initially resisted the approach. It was counter-intuitive."

"Ok. I'm waiting. Go on," said Bob.

"Well, the approach doesn't *start* with saying yes and no. We needed a bit of patience. We, like you, were trying to do everything for everybody. We didn't have any way to determine *what* was most important and equally *who* was most important. We did it all."

"I'm listening."

"Well, we took a step back and looked at the various units and clients we support and we categorized them based on the type of support they required. Knowing that, we were able to work with them to determine *their* highest areas of importance."

"So, if I understand you, what you're saying is the people putting demands on you were asking for everything, in large part, because *they* weren't sure what was critical versus desirable," said Bob.

"Exactly, it was eye opening," replied Bill.

"We make a living by what we get, but we make a life by what we give."

– Winston Churchill

5
Creating Value

The idea of creating value, improving the manner in which you serve others, is not new. The challenge, however, is that today many companies are going broke attempting to provide additional value to their customers. People and organizations are working harder and harder to respond to marketplace demands, yet, in many cases, their actions are providing less and less value.

Today, thanks to a flatter and faster world, serving customers, profitably, is taking on a new level of complexity. It is simply not enough to advocate service and train people, an organization must structurally enable it to occur by streamlining their systems and services. To achieve this, organizations must *proactively* identify their targeted set of customers (current and future), and with that understanding, establish flexible processes that are able to assess and respond to their ever-changing needs and priorities.

This information – targeted customers and their highest-valued needs – will allow an organization or work unit to *proactively* tailor their service levels in order to most effectively and profitably respond to customers and/or internal clients. In addition, they will identify lower-value priorities, which, via technology, outsourcing or new forms of alliances, can be addressed in a more efficient and likely more effective manner. Organizations run the risk of competing agendas and increased bureaucracy when decisions such as these are left up to the varying interpretation of each individual and/or department.

The following chapters will be directed toward specific leadership and individual behaviors that facilitate a value-oriented, service-centric work climate. The remainder of this chapter focuses on how it must be structurally enabled.

Southwest Airlines

If you picked the worst industry in which to compete over the past two decades, it would be the airlines industry. Every airline struggled to make money except one: Southwest.

Virtually all major airlines with the exception of Southwest failed to streamline their systems and services. They failed to align their organizational structure, costs, people and processes around delivering what their customers valued. Instead, they continually resorted to price increases, cost cutting or more recently Chapter 11 protection in order to survive.

While Southwest's success story has been well chronicled, little points to the two most critical factors of their sustained success. First, they discovered what a targeted group of customers – short-distance business travelers – most valued, and second, they diligently aligned their workforce around delivering it.

Every process, person and system in their organization has been engineered to deliver value to their customers and fellow coworkers. Southwest became the most profitable airline because every decision, ranging from what planes they fly to whom they hire, were completely aligned to address the highest valued priorities of short-distance business travelers.

Southwest achieved exceptional financial performance in an industry that typically makes no profit. It is the only major airline in the world that made money consistently every year *for over thirty-years!*

Equally intriguing to Southwest's sustainable performance is their high customer satisfaction level and excellent safety record while maintaining the lowest cost structure in the industry. Southwest continues to have a highly motivated and well-paid workforce, and the airline is continually sought by airport authorities to serve their cities.

Much of the well-deserved credit for Southwest's sustainable success is directed toward the vision, charisma and leadership of former CEO Herb Kelleher. However, more attention should be directed at *what* he did versus *who* he was. It would be extremely difficult to replicate Kelleher's personality and vision; however, his *approach* is reproducible. He structurally aligned Southwest Airlines – strategic focus, business processes, leadership, structure, measures and rewards – around the value they intended to deliver to their targeted customers – short-distance business travelers. In turn, he fostered a sustainable work environment that aligned individuals' passion and skills around serving the needs of their customers and coworkers. Kelleher was able to tap the talent of his employees by providing them with a greater degree of purpose, creativity, teamwork and empowerment. As a result, he built trust and *shared* accountability for end results. The hidden secret behind Southwest's sustainable success is that they enabled a meaningful and productive work environment by delivering value to a targeted set of customers, which in turn, fueled an internal atmosphere of serving each other.

Focusing on the Right Things

Consider a fully expanded balloon, where adding more air would cause it to burst. New air, fresh air, cannot enter the balloon until some of the stale air is first removed. This analogy applies to many organizations. People for the most part are working hard, yet in many cases they may be working on activities that no longer deliver the same degree of value they once did. The stale work remains, yet the *value* the employee and recipients derive from the work is gone.

Many employees and organizations are dealing with stale air. Inconsistent agendas, different interpretations of customer or coworker needs, and lack of prioritization and focus insidiously erodes relationship quality. This in turn erodes employee engagement, creativity, teamwork and productivity. Compensation may temporarily offset the effects of stale air, but not for long. Having good people does not guarantee a strong organization; ensuring good people are focused on the right things does.

Organizations, big and small, spend huge amounts of money attempting to improve organizational productivity and profitability. Significant effort is directed toward improving *current* practices, making the organization leaner by reengineering how the work is done or downsizing the people doing it. While continually improving operational efficiency is necessary, it is far from sufficient.

Customer needs and priorities will shape an organization's purpose, ensuring alignment on the highest valued and most profitable areas. Frustration will be reduced and productivity increased by optimizing or eliminating time, cost and resources directed toward lower-value activities. While this may sound obvious, many organizations struggle trying to serve their customers. They have improved their ability to listen to the voice of their customers; however, they are finding it extremely difficult to respond to it ... *profitably.*

It is the responsibility of every work unit or organization to aggregate, define, anticipate and prioritize the needs of their customers or coworkers. For purposes here, and at the risk of over-simplification, customer and/or coworker needs and priorities can be categorized in the following ways: offering **new things** (products, services, information, etc.); improving the **ease and quality of current things**; and finally, **reducing the cost** of using or acquiring current things. Many employees, or work units, may not directly contribute *new things* (products, services, and information); yet, *everyone* is capable of improving the quality, ease and cost of what they do, *how* they work. When defined in this context, creating and delivering value extends well beyond providing high-quality and cost-effective products and services, it encompasses *how* business is conducted.

Imagine for a minute you own a bike shop. Who are your target customers? Who do you want to attract and cater too? Recreational bikers? Kids? High-performance bikers? These decisions may be based on profitability, your interests and experiences, or possibly based on the demographics of your community. If you decide to target the high performance biker, are you proactively aligned to serve them? Are your employees sensitized to their unique needs? Are they equipped to ask the right questions? Do you offer services tailored to the needs of high-end bikers?

Questions like these must be proactively considered by the owners/leaders of this store. They cannot be left up to the individual discretion of each employee. Answers to these questions will determine the work processes, performance measures, reward systems, and the look and feel for the store. They will define the image you want to convey, the reputation you want to build. The answers define who you will hire and how you will train them.

Organizations who don't address these questions are asking for problems, internally and externally. Internally, they run the risk of employees having different interpretations of the store's focus, their target customers. As such, each employee may operate differently, both with coworkers and customers. Conflicts will surface, and, in time, creativity and cooperation will likely decline. Externally, customers will have different experiences when they visit, call or search your store's website. Word of mouth, the most valuable means of promotion, will be inconsistent. Bad news travels a lot further and faster than good news.

Significant discord and performance related issues can be traced to this lack of customer understanding and focus. In today's turbulent world, people cannot do everything, nor in fact, should they. They require the ability to make consistent and timely trade-off decisions. Leaders' have to enable this to occur. Establishing a shared vision and providing strategic clarity is important, but not enough as it is somewhat periodic in nature. Whereas streamlining systems and services by proactively defining the organization's target customers and identifying their highest priorities and needs facilitates greater operational day-to-day empowerment. This in turn more fully engages employees – head, hands and heart. They will be able to reconcile differences, find common ground and discover creative solutions that add value or eliminate waste. Organizational performance will improve, as will shareholder value, and a more meaningful and productive work climate will ensue.

Segment – Aggregate – Leverage

Many organizations or work units are attempting to be everything to everybody. They are unable to assess importance and differentiate between high- or low-value requests. Not all requests or demands are of equal value, nor are all requestors of equal importance. Similarly, not all customers or coworkers want the same thing or to be treated the same way. Some want a high-touch relationship, while others prefer the opposite. Both are right. The key is for organizations and work units to differentiate and tailor their approach to each while reducing costs, increasing value, and, in the process, regaining a sense of sanity and control.

Each shape in the graphic to the right denotes a different type of customer or internal client. Each shape has different preferences, priorities and temperament. One shape may require assistance and support, while another, due to their familiarity, are comfortable doing it themselves.

The various shapes may buy similar products or require similar services; however, each shape prefers to interact in a different way; the way *they want to be served* varies dramatically. Yet, in most cases, organizations or work units are unable to delineate the difference. Money and time is being wasted, and unfortunately, satisfaction is not being improved. Serving others is not about responding to everything they *want*, it is being able to understand what they *need* and *value*; knowing when to say *yes* and when to say *no*.

Segmentation, as shown here, allows an organization or work unit to proactively categorize those they serve (shapes) into common groups; groups that tend to require similar things in similar ways.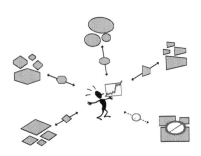

Segmentation allows an organization or work unit to *aggregate* and prioritize their highest-valued needs, and in so doing, *leverage* the manner in which they address them. In this case, rather than seeing hundreds of customers and thousands of discrete requests, a work unit will learn to more effectively serve a small amount (3-5) of customer segments.

Streamlining systems and services allows an organization or work unit to *proactively* align their strategies, work processes, service levels, resources and metrics consistent with the needs of a specific group of customers and/or internal clients that share similar needs. Productivity increases as low-value activities (costs) are optimized, outsourced or eliminated. Innovation goes up as the noise (misaligned expectations) in the relationship is eliminated, and time and resources are concentrated on the real issues, the real needs. Relationship quality and service improves dramatically as mutual expectations are better managed.

For instance, an IT department serves multiple internal clients; however, the needs and priorities of Accounting vary significantly from that of Marketing, Manufacturing or Research. Each internal client at different times, requires new things, and at other times, requires optimization of the things they are already receiving. The same example applies to external customers as the earlier bike store analogy reflected. While certain customers may purchase the same bikes, some may want help with assembly or installation, others may need assistance with high-performance accessories, while still others may want to tailor their purchase – color, size and terms. Likewise in the IT example, having the ability to tailor the approach to each different type of customer is beneficial in terms of cost, profitability and ultimately the value delivered.

Streamlining systems and services does not imply doing everything for everybody. Instead, it provides a proactive way to plan ahead, aligning the appropriate strategies, resources and people necessary to fulfill a particular segment of customers' needs in the most effective and efficient fashion. As the previous graphic suggested, certain segments may be in your best interests *not* to serve. Their needs, expectations and/or operating style may be inconsistent with your ability and/or desire to profitably serve them.

The point is, in order to streamline systems and services, organizations and/or work units must be able to proactively capture, aggregate and analyze the needs of their customers and internal clients. This will allow them to more quickly, profitably and creatively leverage their response to them.

Dow Corning

The earlier Southwest example provides compelling evidence of the benefits of customer-centricity. What is less obvious is the fact that Southwest, due to Kelleher's foresight, has inculcated this mindset into Southwest's culture from their inception. But what about a more common situation where this mindset may not be present in the culture? What about where internal agendas are not well aligned with the external world, and as a result, restrict employees' ability to collectively respond to the demands of customers and coworkers? It is important to compare the Southwest example with an organization that faced issues common to most of today's organizations: escalating costs, eroding profit margins, increasing competitive inroads, and declining morale and customer satisfaction.

With a sixty year history of innovation and market success, Dow Corning required significant transformation of mindsets and business approaches to meet these challenges head on. Strategies and practices that made Dow Corning a leader in the silicone industry were no longer in sync with the dynamics of today's customers and the effects of a rapidly flattening world. The odds of success were certainly not in their favor, considering the fact that they were simultaneously dealing with the effects of Chapter 11 due to breast implant litigation – which makes all the more reason to share their story.

Like many organizations, Dow Corning initially focused on internal cost optimization and re-engineering work processes to improve their operational efficiencies, which certainly helped. However, these changes did not necessarily facilitate growth or workplace improvement. Dow Corning, as many other organizations are discovering, recognized that internal cost-cutting and re-engineering does not ensure long-term sustainability nor spawn growth – financially or emotively. While profitability may have been temporarily improved, not all was well.

Dow Corning learned instead that the answer laid, as it always had, with focusing on delivering increased value to their customers and coworkers, and aligning people and processes accordingly – a concept, far from novel that unfortunately many organizations have lost sight of.

Dow Corning's journey to change the company began in the late 90s when they were facing intense economic pressures. As former CEO Gary Anderson stated in 2002, "Our goal is to provide exactly what customers want, so that they pay only for the products and services they need. We anticipate these changes will provide a key point of differentiation for Dow Corning."

While these changes were guided by their desire to change the way in which they served their customers, in order to do so, Dow Corning needed to transform their corporate culture. Leaders needed to create a work environment that focused on delivering value to their customers by streamlining their systems and service levels, which in turn required workers to focus on the value they provided to their fellow coworkers. Leaders needed to realign personal self-interests and unit priorities with the evolving needs of their customers and/or internal clients – reducing internal silos and/or barriers.

Many of Dow Corning's mature products were no longer novel, and customers were instead seeking ways to cut costs. In response, Dow Corning created an e-based approach to this low-price customer segment and aligned their people and processes accordingly. They reduced their costs, yet, interestingly, *improved* the value they provided to this particular segment of customers. This strategic shift was a counter-intuitive move, one which industry pundits initially questioned. However, now with hindsight in their favor, Dow Corning's actions have proven it is possible to optimize costs and provide additional value while simultaneously improving employee morale and sense of meaning, which is a fact Southwest Airlines has always known.

"Transforming an organizational culture from transactional to more value oriented, something admittedly more nebulous, could not be done with the simplicity of a corporate wide email announcing a new approach," says Marie Eckstein, a Dow Corning global executive director. "Along the way it required actions that challenged the historic culture and personality of Dow Corning. Whether on the frontline of sales or in the often faceless world of manufacturing, employees needed to adopt a more customer-focused approach. We had to aggressively change status quo. Dow Corning is more entrepreneurial, focused and purpose-driven. People are excited about the things we're doing; they feel that they all have a part in making it a success – not just for us, but the customer."

~

This story continues to unfold and it would be premature to claim victory. However, since the spring of 2002, when their new strategy was launched, Dow Corning has experienced significant increases in both top- and bottom-line results – flat during much of the late 90s. While some of their growth was due to acquiring competitive share and the introduction of new products, in large part it was also due to reorienting their culture around creating and delivering increased value, which customers were willing to pay for.

In addition to financial growth, there are additional indications that suggest Dow Corning is heading in the right direction. In 2005, Dow Corning was recognized as one of America's Greatest Brands and was awarded "Specialty Chemical Company of the Year" by *Frost & Sullivan*, a recognized leader in market research. Dow Corning's current CEO, Stephanie Burns, was added to *Forbes* list of most powerful women, and in 2005 (and every year since), *Working Mothers Magazine* acknowledged Dow Corning as one of the 100 Best Companies to work for, and in 2007 *Fortune* magazine did likewise. In addition, the Dow Corning story of enterprise transformation was profiled in a business book published in 2003 by McGraw-Hill entitled *Value Based Marketing for Bottom-Line Success*, which highlighted the steps, from a marketing perspective, taken by Dow Corning to manage this value-based transformation.

While a lot of progress has been made, in many respects the journey is just beginning. *Internally*, Dow Corning has successfully reengineered their strategies, resources and mindsets around their customers. However, as Dow Corning continues to learn more about the needs and expectations of their customers, they are quickly discovering they cannot address them all, especially by themselves. Therefore, the necessity to work differently and more co-creatively with *external* partners takes on increasingly more importance. Sharing knowledge, resources, costs and risks with outside partners will ensure the pipeline of customer value is continually replenished. In addition to improving Dow Corning's economic outlook, these changes better position Dow Corning to compete in a more interconnected and flatter world. Taking an outside-in view, while humbling, has allowed Dow Corning to recognize they are one piece of a much larger puzzle. As result, they respect the need to work differently internally as well as externally with their customers, suppliers, and in some cases, their competitors.

Employees and work units now have a clearer line of sight relative to how they contribute. The workforce has a renewed sense of shared purpose, and internal agendas, systems and service levels are better aligned within the context of delivering value to customers, coworkers and shareholders.

A week later ...

"Bill, I've been thinking about our last discussion about managing expectations."

"And?"

"It is amazing; when you look around there are signs of 'managing expectations' everywhere," replied Bob.

"I'd agree. What are some examples?"

"Insurance. Benefit plans. Delivery services. And we see it every day in retail. As consumers, we're now able to tailor our purchases to meet our needs. If we want overnight shipping, they'll provide it, but it costs us more. If we want our purchases assembled, once again, they'll do it, but it costs us a bit more. Makes sense when you think about it. Not everybody has the same priorities or values the same things."

"I agree," responded Bill. "Healthcare has radically changed its approach. Previously, we'd go through a battery of tests and procedures to diagnose our problems. Now they are far more discerning. In the process, they are likely saving money, but I must say, I actually prefer the more tailored approach."

"Same thing applies to hotels and restaurants. Certain places appeal to certain tastes. They don't try and be everything to everybody. Instead, they focus on attracting a certain clientele, which, I'd imagine, allows them to better align their people and capabilities to serve them."

"I didn't realize how pervasive this thinking really was," replied Bill. "I thought our department stumbled onto something really novel and radical, when in reality, it was reapplying good ol' common sense."

"You're right. It's taking a customer service approach inside the company, where we see each department as a supplier and each internal client as a potential customer. By thinking this way, we can draw upon a number of daily examples to reinforce the approach and thought process," responded Bob.

"In your discussions, did anything surface that hits closer to home? Daily issues that your department is battling?"

"Why do you ask?"

"To build support for change, it wouldn't hurt if you were able to connect it closer to home."

"The significant problems we face cannot be solved by the same level of thinking that created them."

– Albert Einstein

6
Fighting Today's Fires

Many people are reluctant to embrace a changing world, a flatter view of reality. To some, they may believe that global flattening does not pertain to them. For whatever reasons, they believe their business, institution or community is insulated from the effects of market globalization and advances in information technology, or they believe it is possible to delay their response to it. In most situations, this is not due to ignorance, but instead due to more pressing issues. Many leaders and organizations are overwhelmed with fighting today's fires; their immediate concern is surviving in the current world, not necessarily preparing for a flatter one. Given this reality, it is important for leaders to see immediate returns for their time and investment. The more leaders see how a more meaningful and productive work climate, focused on delivering value to coworkers and customers, is the central answer to fighting today's fires, the more they will be inclined to pursue it.

Shifting workforce focus toward creating and delivering value will continue to increase *profitability* by eliminating or optimizing low-value activities, yet it also provides an infinite source of *motivation* to the employees. They proactively assume responsibility for their own fate by continually assessing and refining the value they, or their team, offer to others. By shifting emphasis toward value delivery, people are more inclined to work *collaboratively* with others in order to increase the value they can collectively deliver. In today's world, problems are increasingly more complex. It is rare that any one individual or organization, with access to the very same information, will arrive at the same conclusions. There are a lot of good ideas that never get implemented. In many cases, failure was not due to the quality of the idea, but due to the reluctance to include others in a co-creative and collaborative process.

While the world is becoming smaller and flatter, in reality, at the personal level, it is becoming bigger and more complex. People can no longer focus narrowly on their local interests, ignoring global realities. By emphasizing value creation and delivery, a greater and more dynamic degree of *creativity* will result. Creative differences and/or divergent perspectives, when shared in the context of how each contributes value, have a better chance of being reconciled. Synergies will more easily surface, as will greater emphasis on collaboration due to recognition of the interdependent nature of today's problem solving. Answers, in today's flatter and more complex world, will result from cross-breeding not inbreeding.

Organizations must be both *resilient* and *responsive*. Their left hand has to be able to deliver what their right hand promises. Unfortunately, this is the exact opposite of what many customers experience. While an organization's right hand is willing to make commitments to acquire a customer's business, the left hand (people and processes) has difficulty fulfilling it or, in many cases, doing it profitably. By understanding what a customer and/or coworker really values, it allows an organization or work unit to focus on doing the right things and optimizes or eliminates time and money spent doing the wrong things. Increased satisfaction is *not* a result of doing everything customers or coworkers *want*, instead it is improved by understanding and delivering what they *need*.

Productive organizations and/or work units cannot afford to be everything to everybody. Success is not a result of doing everything, but instead a result of focusing on what is most important and valued. This implies that individuals and organizations must take an *active* interest in understanding the needs and priorities of those they serve, coworkers and customers, and understand what keeps them up at night. What concerns, issues or opportunities are *they* in the throes of dealing with? As a result, by understanding their highest priorities, employees, personally and collectively, can more effectively align their capabilities to respond to them. In the process, more value is created, costs are optimized and *quality* improves, often with less work. The distractions (low-value activities) will be eliminated from the relationship by focusing on the real needs, the real issues. It no longer is a question of attempting to do everything; instead, it is a passion around doing the *right* things.

Health Care

An example, in a rather visible industry, will help illustrate the points made above.

According to the Center for Disease Control more than 50% of the two trillion dollars spent annually on healthcare is avoidable. Recognizing this, healthcare providers – in particular, hospitals – must transform themselves. To remain viable, hospitals need to reduce internal silos, increase consumer focus and eliminate process bottlenecks; they must redefine historic boundaries in order to improve consumer value.

Although this is not easy, it's possible. For example, ThedaCare, in Appleton, Wisconsin, is among U.S. leaders at optimizing consumer value, with the goal of rethinking, simplifying, streamlining and standardizing how they care for patients. Guy Boulton, in an online article posted in March, 2008 (journalsentinel.com), wrote "their drive to improve value is similar to what occurred in the manufacturing sector in the 90s, drawing upon "process improvement" techniques as a means to optimize costs and generate value." ThedaCare estimates that in 2005 and 2006 they cut costs by $22 million a year, without layoffs, while reducing medical errors. They've shown that lower costs do not result in lower quality, with a mortality rate due to bypass surgeries that beats national benchmarks.

In many cases, identifying new sources of value is a result of expanding our perspective. Today, for example, when considering care delivery, most attention is directed to the actual provision of care – diagnosis, tests, treatment, etc.

This assumes that as long as hospitals provide competent staff and apply proven practices they will achieve good results in terms of health and overall patient value.

If this is the extent in which they consider the care delivery *process*, these views may seem accurate; however, when viewed from the eyes of the patient, they are rather limiting. Data from survey firms such as Press Ganey suggest there are many other factors that determine patient satisfaction and overall value, some that occur prior to treatment, others that occur during or post-treatment.

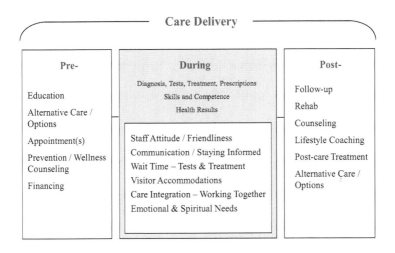

Such things as education, alternative care or financing options may be important prior to receiving treatment, each providing additional opportunities for value creation. Whereas, in addition to receiving quality care during treatment, patients are also affected by such things as staff attitude, staying informed, wait times, patient transport and visitor accommodations. Following treatment, overall patient value can be increased by addressing activities such as follow-up, counseling and after-care services. All of these factors – pre, during and post – provide opportunities for value creation and work process optimization, if and when viewed from the eyes of the consumer or patient.

In this example, by emphasizing consumer value, productivity will be improved, as will innovation, responsiveness and quality. The work climate will also be improved, allowing people to extract more meaning from their jobs. In their book, *Redefining Health Care: Creating a Value-Based Competition on Results (2006)*, authors, Porter and Teisberg stated that "the goal of improving value for patients will unite the interests of system participants who now too often work at cross purposes. When all parties compete to achieve the best medical outcomes for patients, they are pursuing the goals that led many individuals into the profession in the first place."

A few days later ...

"Bill, you were right."

"How's that?"

"I asked people to look closer at issues that are affecting us on a daily basis."

"Discover anything?"

"Lots. Virtually everything is affected. By taking a proactive interest in our clients' needs, and better managing their expectations, we will need to evolve as their needs evolve. We need to provide new or optimized services that support their evolution versus being blind to it, eliminating activities that are no longer valued. Sounds obvious, but frankly these discussions have helped us realize that we have lost touch with our clients. A lot of our attention has been directed toward internal issues and agendas."

"I would agree."

"Bill, I have to run, but first let me ask you something. We've talked a lot about the changes your department has made and how it has personally impacted you. I'm curious, how has it affected your department leaders? During this process, have you noticed much difference in them? Has their approach changed?"

"In a word Bob – dramatically! Previously they had a very forceful approach. They told us what to do and how to do it. In addition, they changed their minds quite frequently. It caused a lot of grief, and employees were unhappy and demoralized. They didn't seem to be interested in our ideas or suggestions, so many of us simply tuned out."

"Interesting, go on," stated Bob, as he was recognizing the same leadership traits within his department.

"Well, since our changes, their style has evolved dramatically. We are all more unified and, this may sound odd, but there is more of a collegial attitude within our department. People are feeling more valued and our ideas and suggestions seem welcomed, actually sought out unlike before."

"Was there much turnover? Did you have to change many of the previous leaders given your recent improvements?"

"A few, but not many. In hindsight, it was obvious many of the leaders were equally frustrated with how our department was operating. And many of them were feeling the heat, not only from us employees, but also from upper-management. Suffice to say, it wasn't enjoyable for anybody. Bob, realize I'm able to say this now, but I certainly didn't fully comprehend it at the time."

"I understand. Actually I'm glad I asked the question. It's very encouraging to listen to what you're saying. Let's catch-up later, I'd like to continue this conversation, particularly the topic of leadership."

"Transformation in thinking from 'I' to 'we' is the most important process leaders go through in becoming authentic. Only when leaders stop focusing on their personal ego needs are they able to develop other leaders ... they recognize the unlimited potential of empowered leaders working together toward a shared purpose."

– Bill George, Author
True North

7
Transformational Leadership

"As for the best leaders, the people do not notice their existence. The next best, the people honor and praise. The next, the people respect; and the next, the people fear and hate. When the best leader's work is done, the people say, 'We did it ourselves.'"

- Lao-Tzu (Chinese philosopher)

Everyone and every job has an element of leadership attached to it; some more than others. While task knowledge, problem solving and track record may be what initially secures a leadership position, communication, empathy, focus and shared-accountability are some of the traits that will determine how effective a leader is.

As individuals we can and should take pride in our work and accomplishments; however, as leaders, similar to parents, we should take personal pride in the accomplishments of *others*. As the quote above suggests, BEST leaders go unnoticed because the people will say they did it themselves. This is interesting, and rather counter-intuitive, especially in America. If true, it's quite possible that personality traits that reflect good leaders, such as charisma, power and status, may be the very same traits that prevent good leaders from becoming the BEST ones.

As previously stated, this book is directed toward the characteristics of the BEST leaders; those individuals capable of continually delivering results by instilling commitment versus compliance within their workforce. People have unlimited capacity, and BEST leaders create an environment that allows them to discover and tap it.

Engaged and motivated employees require more than fair pay, career growth and safe working conditions. By providing employees a better line-of-sight relative to how they or their work units contribute value, leaders will be triggering intrinsic motivators, which in turn will result in more committed and engaged employees. Expectations can be better managed and, as a result, relationship quality, productivity, creativity and teamwork will improve. Conflicting agendas and self-interests are resolved in the context of a shared purpose that aligns individual agendas with organizational priorities; organizational priorities that are focused on delivering value.

Noel M. Tichy, in his book *The Leadership Engine*, stated "companies can win only if they quickly deliver the goods and services that customers want … they must be willing to tailor their products and delivery schedules to respond to individual customer needs … this requires an organization that isn't built to last but one that is built to change." He went on to say "the real core competence of companies will be the ability to continuously and creatively destroy and remake themselves to meet customer demands."

For this to occur paradigms must be shifted, and beliefs, mindsets and work practices must be redefined. The global marketplace will continue to evolve and change, therefore, today's organizations must be able to evolve and grow. This implies that leaders must be skilled at leading change. In addition to developing their own personal resiliency and self-awareness, they must be equipped – intellectually and emotionally – to lead others through the turbulence of a changing world. Their ability to deliver bottom-line results is dependent on it, as is the sanity, effectiveness and sense of hope of those they lead.

In the Introduction, BEST leaders were characterized as leaders who **B**uild trust and accountability; **E**stablish shared purpose; **S**treamline systems and services; **T**ap talent. In large part, the ability to build trust and accountability and tap talent is a result of establishing shared purpose and streamlining systems and services; thus the focus of this book. The earlier chapter, *Creating Value*, addressed streamlining systems and services; whereas what immediately follows focuses on the importance of establishing shared purpose.

Establishing Shared Purpose

In order to achieve optimum performance, the following bell curve identifies a "zone" we should all strive for, personally and collectively.

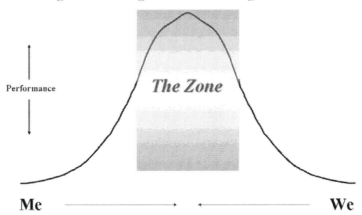

High Performing and Resilient Organizations

Neither extreme is healthy. One extreme, due to self-absorption, results in people failing to see, or even care about the needs of others. Those at the other extreme run the risk of losing themselves and their self-identity in the process. They are so focused on serving the needs of others that they fail to address their *own* needs, to uncover who they really are. Therefore, the answer lies in the middle.

BEST leaders establish a shared purpose for their team or department. While somewhat static, establishing a vision, mission, and strategic objectives is an excellent place to start. However, in order to achieve workforce alignment with the ever-changing needs and pace of today's marketplace, leaders must better align their workforce with the needs and priorities of those they serve, how they deliver value to internal or external clients or customers. The following represent just a few reasons why.

<u>One</u> – Expectations continually change – they must. Therefore, individuals must be equipped to change with them. Given this expanded view of reality, people need to continually shape and/or redefine *who* they are, *what* they provide. They need to embrace new insights and divergent perspectives and, in the process, be willing to discard existing practices or beliefs that are no longer appropriate. The workplace is filled with people who have never developed the life skills or agility in dealing with continually shifting expectations, external influences, self versus shared interests, conflict and opposition, and the variety and pace of choices the workplace offers daily. People in today's individualistic world tend to be more focused on defending their self-interests rather than considering the shared interests of the larger organization. If each person or department had a better understanding of the higher or shared purpose – delivering value to customers and coworkers and how they personally contribute to it – their ability to reconcile self-

interests and manage expectations and commitments would become easier.

<u>Two</u> – As outlined throughout this book, people are more inspired and engaged when they can see how *they* personally contribute value to others. While achieving strategic priorities and three-year plans are extremely relevant to organizational leaders, most people are not necessarily motivated by the same experience.

<u>Three</u> – Strategies and objectives, even well-crafted ones, change before the ink dries. Why? Because the needs and priorities of customers and coworkers continually change, especially given today's real-time access to information. It is reality that is difficult to deny and naive to ignore. There is virtually no way that strategies and objectives can be modified to reflect the pace of change. Likewise, even the most skilled leaders will not be able to keep pace with continually shifting expectations, reconciling one fire only to discover additional fires continually surfacing. Therefore, it behooves leaders to align their people closer to the *source* of these changes – their external and internal clients. They must teach and/or empower them to capture, analyze, and react to shifting needs and priorities. Strategies and objectives provide focus and decision-making latitudes; however, every individual must assume increased and shared accountability for results as measured by the value created and delivered to those people they serve.

<u>Four</u> – improving productivity, creativity and quality. The key to the quality movements of the 80s and 90s was to better align decision making to those individuals closer to operational realities. As a result, this empowered people to act and react in a timely fashion and, in the process, instilled a stronger degree of ownership and shared accountability for results. Employees were taught how to read, analyze and react to changing conditions. The same concept

applies here. Business conditions are continually fluctuating, which in turn cause needs and priorities of customers and coworkers to continually fluctuate. As a result, individuals and departments need to be better equipped to fluctuate with them.

Five – Cross team/department resolution. The previous four points are necessary to improve intra-team performance, but they are also essential to improve *inter*-team performance. As organizations become flatter, many supervisors' span of control is widening and they are responsible for a greater number of people, hence, issues. Therefore, a personally-intimate approach that may have worked when supervisors were responsible for less people or when the pace of change was slower, no longer works. Consider the fact that the performance of most teams is dependent on how well they interact with other teams or departments, and how well they manage interdependencies, commitments and trade-offs. If each "team" is dependent on its leader to reconcile commitments or differences with other leaders – keeping in mind the pace and complexity in today's business climate – a bottleneck will naturally occur. Leaders can only do so much, especially when you consider their broadening span of responsibility. Individuals and teams, rather than relying on leaders to reconcile differences, should learn to use the needs and priorities of their customers as their North Star. In the process, it will become clearer how each team or individual does or does not contribute value. The debate is no longer between individual viewpoints or self-interests. Instead, healthy debate occurs within the shared context of delivering value.

A Whole New Mind

Daniel H. Pink, author of *A Whole New Mind: Moving from the Information Age to the Conceptual Age*, wrote how the Industrial

Age relied on manual skills and was followed by the Information Age, which was dependent upon knowledge and intelligence or left-brain characteristics. He feels we are now entering the Conceptual Age, which puts a premium on creativity and integrative skills. Mr. Pink reported that IQ accounts for 4-10 percent of career success after examining a number of academic studies that attempted to measure it. Pink stated, "Today, the defining skills of the previous era – the 'left brain' capabilities that powered the Information Age – are necessary but no longer sufficient. And the capabilities we once ordained or thought frivolous – the 'right-brain' qualities of inventiveness, empathy, joyfulness, and meaning – increasingly will determine who flourishes and who flounders." He felt, "Left-brain thinking has resulted in prosperity and abundance; however, ironically, prosperity has now placed a premium on less rational and more emotive or right-brain characteristics. For businesses, it's no longer enough to create a product that's reasonably priced and adequately functional. It must also be beautiful, unique, and meaningful." He went on to state, "The high-concept abilities of an artist are often more valuable than the easily replicated left-brain skills of an entry-level business graduate."

With that said, today's left-brain leaders don't necessarily have to experience a psychological overhaul to be effective. They can structurally enable a right-brain work environment by broadening and transforming employee understanding as to how they or their department align with organizational priorities and contribute value – the frequently repeated message of this book. For commitment and loyalty to improve, people must first be focused on the right things, those things that result in value to others, not diminish it. By doing so, their strengths and contributions will be visible, as will their blind spots and weaknesses. In essence, they will become more self-aware, which is a prerequisite for personal growth and for valuing the interdependency and contribution of others. As a result employees will become emotionally connected and committed to each other and to what they do.

Managing Transition

In today's world, change is not optional. As Tichy stated earlier, "the real core competence of companies will be the ability to continuously and creatively destroy and remake themselves to meet customer demands." This is easier said than done. Many organizations clumsily pursue change, slowly eroding trust, relationship quality and degree of collaboration. Similar to how water slowly erodes or alters the environmental landscape, poor execution of organizational change does the same to the organizational landscape. With that in mind, as organizations strive to become more value-based – instilling a more dynamic, service-oriented work climate – they will also have to become skilled at continuously remaking themselves.

Leading change can be compared to that of raising a child, better yet a teenager. During the pre-teen years, a parent *usually* has far more control and influence over both the actions of the child and the social situations the child is exposed to. The child is far more dependent on their parents, realizing that by themselves they are not equipped to tackle the world alone. Parents lead and the child typically follows.

However, this dependence begins to change as children approach their teenage years. A teenager's self-identity (independence) is formed, in many ways challenging the shared interests of the family or parents. A parent's role, especially during these critical years, is to help the child learn how to achieve balance between their self interests and the shared interests of others. Some parents achieve this and some do not. Although parenting might appear as a series of events, in reality it is a process, a process with a destination in mind – raising responsible and resilient adults. It is also a process in which the parent does not have complete control over. Teenagers are exposed to external influences, good and bad, that shape their behavior, their decisions, and their growth.

Welcome to the world of leading change ...

The workplace is filled with people who have never developed the skills or agility in dealing with continually shifting expectations and external influences. The speed of globalization and technology advances acts as a flame beneath the pot, whereas the individual challenges articulated just above are amplified the more the heat is turned up. As a result, many well-intentioned change initiatives fail to achieve or sustain the intended results – performance suffers, leaders become frustrated, and employees grow weary and cynical.

Many leaders get frustrated with individuals' unwillingness to change. They see resistance as a form of rejection of the proposed change versus simply a person's or group's way of expressing uneasiness with the personal risk and/or discomfort involved in going there. As a result of missing this simple fact, leaders spend an inordinate amount of time attempting to convince people of the proposed benefits and/or forcing their employees to embrace them.

Transition – abandoning historic practices and beliefs in order to embrace new ones – is not a desirable place to be, but going through it cannot be avoided. Experiencing transition is uncomfortable; people lose their previous sense of control, and conflict and stress increases. While people must be led through this state of transition, they do not want to remain there very long. We've all heard the saying 'as one door closes another will open;' however this cliché fails to mention that it's hell in the hallway.

The more leaders understand the dynamics of transition, the more successful they will be at leading people into and through it. As a result, the more successful they will be at leading change, which in today's dynamic business climate is a significant competitive advantage.

Leading change has less to do with the brilliance of an idea and more to do with how the proposed change aligns with an organization's culture and strategies and/or the degree in which the change disrupts current norms, beliefs and practices. Therefore, while a key element to managing change has to do with defining *what* the change entails, even greater emphasis should be directed at *how* it's implemented.

In any new initiative, significant time and money are directed toward *content* design. For example, this book provides an overview of what creating a value-based workplace entails – the content. To pursue this change, teams would need to be established, best practices further studied, methods and timelines developed, and concepts would need to be piloted and implemented. Once again, this is all content, focusing on *what* is required. This is all appropriate yet insufficient. Given today's complexities, attention must also be directed toward the situational *context* in which an initiative *fits*. Although it is a relatively minor element when compared to content design and overall cost, assessing *contextual fit* actually plays a disproportionate role in the realization of desired benefits and return on investment. While concepts – such as those presented in this book – may be somewhat universal and/or proven elsewhere, your success will be largely determined by your ability to tailor or "fit" these concepts into your reality, your situational context. Maybe, in your situation, you have trusted leaders skilled at managing change. Great, but that might not be the same elsewhere or even in other departments within the same organization. Maybe, in your situation, you have common work methods and measures already in place, where incorporating a value-based mindset complements pre-existing structures, beliefs and practices. Maybe, in your situation, you have an adaptable workforce skilled at embracing new ideas. The point is, in order for leaders to be effective at leading change they must respect their situational reality. This will help them determine what fits and what doesn't, based on their situation, their priorities, and their budget.

Leading change can be compared to sailing *against* the wind, where agility and tact, reading and reacting to the *contextual* winds of the organization, are extremely important skills. Although there are some exceptions, many organizations do not necessarily welcome change or the individuals who advocate it. Many people with great ideas often lack the personal skills, agility, courage or perseverance to effectively navigate through the organizational winds. Cultural beliefs, existing power structures and historic practices are difficult hurdles to overcome. Yet, to remain healthy, organizations are dependent on the creative, even disruptive, ideas of their people. However, with that said, it takes courageous, skilled and principled individuals – leaders' in the truest form – to stand up for what they believe, especially in the face of significant opposition.

A week later ...

"Bill, last week you touched on the subject of leadership. I have a question for you."

"What's that?"

"From my perspective, it seems that our leaders aren't always on the same page. They have different and often times conflicting priorities."

"I'm not surprised. We were experiencing the same thing. What's your question?"

"How did your department address this?"

"Bob, I'm not sure I know. Like you, for years we had a mission statement and our leaders periodically agreed on priorities, but something certainly changed. "

"Any idea what?"

"Well, like we've been discussing all along, we definitely became more customer focused. Previously, we were working hard, but now we are working smarter, more focused, more unified."

"That makes sense, but how did it actually happen? What changed?"

"I wish I knew," replied Bill, "it was never really clear to me how it actually happened."

"A transformational leader will develop a plan of action, mobilize the workforce, and unleash power by vocalizing the core values of the system."

– Robert E. Quinn, Author
Deep Change

8
The Rest of the Story

The earlier Dow Corning story shared outcomes; financial and cultural outcomes that were achieved as a result of reawakening a value-based business approach. This story is logical, relevant, and to a degree, compelling. Unfortunately, it clouds reality; it's too clean. My intent in this chapter is to revisit this story, drill a bit deeper, and get a little personal.

Value-based transformation, deep change, takes time. The big, visible steps are usually preceded by a series of small, frequently overlooked steps. These smaller steps challenge cultural norms by chipping away at historic beliefs, paradigms and power structures. Similar to how machetes cut through dense jungle foliage, these smaller steps cut through cultural foliage, preparing the way for big changes to follow. The earlier story of Dow Corning reflected the big step, what follows will reflect some of the smaller steps that preceded it, steps that I had the opportunity to lead.

The Missing Piece

Leadership, as depicted here, is a balancing act. Simply said, leaders are equally responsible for financial performance, workplace quality and effectiveness, and customer (or internal client) satisfaction.

85

Organizations, continually, seek ways to improve the overall health of their triangle. To remain relevant, they must. This was certainly the case at Dow Corning. They, in response to competitive pressures and a flattening world, wanted to radically improve performance. In this quest, there was a degree of historical comfort, therefore a lot of emphasis, dealing with two elements of the triangle – financial performance and workforce effectiveness. Financially, a great deal of attention was focused on cost-cutting, yes, even downsizing. And, relative to workforce effectiveness, significant resources were aimed at improving productivity. HR practices were reengineered, supply-chains optimized, product development processes reconstructed, and the organizational structure was overhauled. It was a busy place!

All of these efforts contributed to the story shared in an earlier chapter; however, in order to become a more value-based, customer-focused organization, the third element, the customer, also had to be addressed. That's where, for purposes here, the rest of the story begins.

A Fish Out of Water

Dow Corning cared deeply about their customers. They pioneered a novel technology and over sixty-years, established strong relationships across a multitude of industries and geographies. Yet, thanks to material alternatives, advances in information technology and new forms of competition, times were changing and customers were faced with many options.

I experienced this change first-hand. After spending my first ten years with Dow Corning in internal, back-office roles, I relocated into sales, interfacing directly with our customers. For nearly seven years I had the opportunity to work directly with Dow

Corning's top customer. They were big, complex, interesting, dynamic, and most of all, demanding. They expected a lot and we worked hard to provide it; too hard, however. During this time, I discovered that when our front-office – what we promised – was out of sync with our back-office – what we were able to deliver – we had problems. Not because we didn't care, but because we didn't share. As a result, our triangle was underperforming. Our financial potential fell short, the customer wasn't satisfied, and our workforce effectiveness, in terms of responsiveness, productivity and innovation, suffered. From my rather unique vantage point, if this was occurring with our top customer, I could only imagine what the triangle must have looked like with our other customers.

Back to Base

Initially, naively, I believed I could invoke the necessary cultural changes from my remote sales location. Using the customer's voice (did I say it was one of our most important customers?) to wakeup the organization, constructively surfacing what we needed to change. It didn't work. The challenges were too deep. Realizing that, it became abundantly clear that I needed to return to Base (headquarters), leaving behind my autonomy and company car … but not my voice.

Upon returning to Base, I brought conviction but not necessarily a plan. Initially, I had hoped to validate and confirm my sales observations that there was a breakdown between the front- and back-office. In actuality, it was just the opposite. Either people were content with status quo and/or they relegated "customer service" to those few people on the front-lines that processed orders and handled complaints. In this way, albeit unconsciously, they were deflecting their personal or departmental responsibility in adding value; overlooking perpetual opportunities to reinvent, optimize or eliminate how they served others, inside and outside the organization.

Personally, this was disheartening. I returned to Base with the hope of launching a change train, addressing the ills I experienced while in sales; however, instead, I was humbled. I recognized that my voice alone was not enough to raise awareness and invoke change … it needed to be joined with others and become louder.

Establishing a Shared Voice

Dow Corning was not much different than many other multi-national organizations in that it is rather complex. They had existing power structures, organizational silos, functional disciplines, and served a variety of market sectors globally. Specific to them, they had approximately eight thousand employees, multiple locations, and numerous business units, each aimed at the needs of specific industries such as construction, personal care, automotive, electronics and health care. Depending how you counted them, Dow Corning had over fifteen-thousand customers, spanning multiple product lines, with approximately fifty-percent of their business conducted outside the United States.

Given this complexity and the internal issues it generates, it's not surprising that they struggled staying in tune with the external world, the evolving and dynamic needs of their customers. With this organizational context in mind, the challenge remained: how to establish a "louder" voice; a shared voice that reflected how to best serve our customers. Everybody across business units, regions and disciplines, had a different interpretation of what that meant. I mean everybody! Even fellow sales people – approximately four hundred globally – had various opinions on how to best serve our customers. All of them were right, yet *all of them* created confusion and therefore a lack of cohesion and consistency. Internally, this lack of cohesion negatively affected financial performance and workforce effectiveness, and externally it diluted Dow Corning's success and image in the marketplace.

While this was a global challenge, I personally was located in the U.S. Therefore this presented the logical place to start; a start that spanned approximately nine months. First, industry leaders needed to be made aware of this lack of cohesion or shared voice, and the negative impact it was having on growth, profitability, image and customer relationships. After securing their support, this allowed me to organize a diverse team made up of sales managers and sales professionals, encompassing a cross-section of the industries we served. What followed, without getting into the details, was a multi-step process. We would meet as a group, consider the relevance of existing best practices, merge ideas, and between meetings seek the broader input and/or validation of others. This process started with polar opposition as to our ability to identify commonalities, commonalities that hardhat industries like construction and the cosmetic world of personal care shared. In hindsight, defining the "words" was rather easy, and probably could have been done in one meeting; however, establishing a shared commitment to those words is what took time and patience. In the end, it worked.

This process established a shared-voice, an expanded view of what it took to effectively serve our customers. This expanded view helped build consistency across industries and raised front- and back-office understanding as to their interdependent role in contributing value. It influenced training and work processes, and ultimately, changed the reward systems that existed within sales – moving away from simply rewarding product sales to now having fifty-percent of job performance based on other, newly defined factors. Factors such as relationship building, resource orchestration, strategic alignment, and the ability to position and capture the overall value we provided our customers, beyond product.

Over the next year this process – establishing a shared voice – joined with others and became louder. It was embraced and replicated in both Europe and Asia – more efficiently, I might add, based on what I learned in the U.S. In many respects, each region started with a blank sheet of paper which allowed them to define what "they" believed were the critical factors in serving customers. Conducted this way, the process drew upon the universal nature of people. While both Europe and Asia may have initially articulated their views differently – based upon cultural nuances – their intentions proved identical, which made it rather easy to blend their views into the factors previously developed in the U.S.

This process converted noise into a shared voice; a voice that the rest of the organization could hear and respond to. The conclusions were not novel, but the fact that these conclusions were collectively and globally shared was. This process allowed Dow Corning to **B**uild greater trust and accountability by **E**stablishing a sense of shared purpose, **S**treamlining the systems and services necessary to achieve it, and **T**apping the diverse talents within their workforce. This BEST approach will continue to repeat itself in the steps that immediately follow and was also the approach that resulted in the story shared in an earlier chapter.

Looking Out For Number One

While establishing a shared voice helped to strengthen the customer piece of the triangle, the conclusions it reached also surfaced our next-step – looking out for number one.

Virtually all organizations experience the Pareto effect, where approximately twenty-percent of customers represent eighty-percent of their success. Realizing this, it is wise to stay close to their needs and priorities, real close. These "key" customers may represent significant revenue, may be leaders within their industry, or may be willing to share the risk in pioneering new applications.

In the case of Dow Corning, after leading a rather lengthy and grueling process of gaining agreement on what constituted a key customer, we finally arrived in a position of improving how we interacted with them. To achieve this, however, I first needed to define and gain agreement on how we would serve them. While I led this activity, drawing upon my previous sales experience, it was a team effort. In short, by facilitating multi-area input – in essence, repeating the approach that succeeded in establishing a shared voice – we eventually integrated diverse views and agreed upon a "shared" approach, globally.

Once the process was defined, we shifted our attention on execution. We concentrated initially on a handful of key customers, established global, multi-discipline teams for each one, and assigned a corporate executive to each of these customer teams. In the short course of time, as expected, the realities of serving this type of customer began to surface. Or, stated differently, our weaknesses were exposed. Yet, unlike my time in sales, this occurred in a manner in which their "voices" could be heard and responded to. In this scenario, our top executives, who historically had limited or superficial contact with our customers, were being directly exposed to marketplace realities, the effects of a flatter, more interconnected economy. As a result, they and the cross-discipline, multi-area teams, became more sensitized and therefore more responsive to the cultural changes that needed to occur within Dow Corning. Outwardly, this process was directed at improving performance, particularly financial performance; inwardly it further strengthened the customer piece of the triangle – amplifying the voice of our customers, in this case our most important customers.

By *looking out for number one* the customer's "voice" was becoming louder, but a question still remained … *what do we do about the rest of our customers?*

Service Level Differentiation

While it made perfect sense to improve the manner in which we served our key customers, we could not afford to serve all other customers – the other eighty to ninety percent – in a similar fashion.

The prior step – looking out for number one – improved strategic alignment and front- and back-office cooperation, which, as a result, addressed some of the breakdowns I had personally experienced while in sales. However, it didn't result in the cultural overhaul I had hoped for because it affected a very small amount of the Dow Corning population – those people who had direct contact with our limited number of key customers. While the prior step made a positive dent in the existing culture, the step I'm about to describe – service level differentiation – reinvented it.

Dow Corning had thousands of customers, a small percentage of which were impacted by the key customer processes outlined above. Regardless of size or stature, people are people; they want to be treated with respect, care and consideration. They want to feel special, even unique. To achieve this in today's world means providing choices. The key, therefore, is how to serve these customers, provide them choices, and yet achieve it in a profitable, sustainable manner.

Earlier, in the *Creating Value* chapter, I introduced the concepts of segmentation and service differentiation. My intent here is to briefly show how we applied them within Dow Corning.

As with both steps previously outlined, considering Dow Corning's industry and geographic breadth, it was initially very difficult to find customer similarities across markets. For example, customers within the construction industry required different products, information and support than automotive customers. Going even further, customers in the United States, more experienced with Dow Corning's offerings, required different levels of support than customers based in Asia. Fortunately, after a series of pilots conducted within the various industry units, we discovered the answer. When we considered what the customer *required*, it was virtually impossible to find similarities; however, when we considered how the customer wanted to be *served*, how they preferred to interact, we found similarities that spanned all industries, all cultures.

For example, Dow Corning had customers that preferred to do-it-themselves; others who wanted access to standard, off-the-shelf materials; and still others who wanted tailored choices, materials and/or services customized to their tastes. These "segments," when viewed this way, were universal, regardless of industry or region. Recognizing this consistency, it was then left up to the discretion of each industry and/or region to determine how to best *serve* each of these customer segments. By simplifying how Dow Corning viewed their customers, it helped them proactively, and more effectively align back-office resources. And, in addition, they were able to improve their profitability and strengthen their external image by differentiating their products and services in a manner best conducive to one segment versus another.

Earlier, I mentioned how Dow Corning was predisposed to focus on two elements of the triangle – financial performance and workplace effectiveness. In large part, this was due to a science-based, left-brain mentality where data and facts drove decisions, actions and investments. In contrast, historically, serving customers was considered more of an art versus a science; therefore not well understood. This step – service level differentiation – helped to systematize how Dow Corning saw their customers. By segmenting customers, based on buying preferences, we were able to capture, aggregate and analyze market signals – proactively improving our ability to listen and respond to the voice of our customers. We converted an art into a science, which spoke well in a predominately left-brain world.

In addition, by strengthening the customer piece of the triangle, we were able to connect numerous, disconnected change initiatives under a common umbrella – establishing a greater sense of shared purpose on a corporate scale. Improvement initiatives like six-sigma and e-business, and even difficult decisions such as downsizing or restructuring could now be shown in the context of how they improved our ability to differentiate our service levels. We emphasized "customer" value versus "shareholder" value, which laid the foundation of the story shared in the earlier chapter.

Those Who Serve, Prosper

The intent, in each step outlined in this chapter, was not to share all nuances, obstacles or details, but instead provide a brief glimpse at some of the "smaller" steps that preceded the bigger step I shared in an earlier chapter. Each of these small steps – rather large when you're in the midst of them – helped develop and strengthen the customer piece of the organizational triangle – *simultaneously* improving financial performance, workforce effectiveness and customer value. In a manner of speaking, these steps helped Dow Corning reclaim the essence of business – creating and delivering value to those they served – *Bringing Meaning into Monday* by simultaneously addressing both sides of the same coin – performance and people.

The preceding steps, while initially applied in a rather large, multinational company, have been subsequently reapplied within much smaller, more centralized organizations, both for-profit and not-for-profit.

For example, a small, single location financial planning organization was seeking ways to improve the health of their triangle, particularly workforce effectiveness and back-office productivity. In working with them, they quickly discovered that a significant part of the answer resided within their front-office – in this case, the financial planners that directly interfaced with their external clients.

They, like Dow Corning, had to establish a shared voice, agree on how to best serve their most important clients, and learn how to differentiate their service offerings in order to remain relevant and profitable.

This chapter – actually this book – can be summarized by revisiting the earlier organizational triangle.

1. Leaders must first understand the needs of their customers and/or internal clients. And, as necessary, improve upon their ability to hear and respond to this "voice."

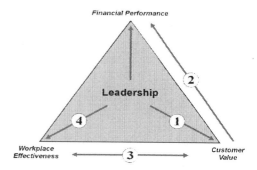

2. Financial performance, in terms of profitability, innovation and growth, will directly improve the more leaders understand this customer piece and tailor their approach to serving it.

3. By understanding the needs of their customers, leaders will be in a better position to proactively align their workforce. This will improve workforce effectiveness, productivity, and overall sense of meaning in terms of cooperation, creativity, sense of contribution, and relationship quality

4. Finally, leaders will discover that the needs of their customers are quite dynamic, especially today. Therefore they will need to better enable and empower their workforce in order to respond. To achieve this they must establish a sense of shared purpose (in this case, by better aligning with the customer piece of the triangle) and streamline the systems, services and work processes necessary to achieve it. As a result, they will be in a better position to tap the talent within and outside the organization, and build trust and increased accountability for results. In this way, good leaders become BEST leaders.

Later that week ...

 "Bill, I'm curious. Do you also find that this greater sense of team or community makes you more resilient? Are you able to deal more effectively with the accelerating pace of change?"

"That's an interesting question, very insightful. Matter of fact, this might be the most significant area of improvement."

"How's that?"

"Well Bob, before we made the changes it seemed that the pace of work was overwhelming us. Everybody was working extremely hard, yet we never seemed to get ahead."

"Go on."

"For instance, I'd personally be so busy and focused on my own activities I'd be hesitant to assist with someone else's and vice versa. We all had our heads down and blinders on."

"Bill, I can relate, however, it's hard to help someone else when it means you'll fall behind on your own work. I'm willing to help others, but it seems I never have the time."

"That *was* also my view. But I stress *was*. I previously thought I knew my job; therefore I didn't always value other people's inputs. However, since we've established a sense of shared purpose within our department, people are far more open to share their unique views. Unlike before, the difference now is they are able to share them within the context of how they contribute to the common goals we share."

"Interesting."

"Personally, by utilizing others," continued Bill, "I've been able to produce far more and I've found numerous work process improvements that I didn't previously recognize."

"Management must be happy?"

"No kidding. What's even better is we now see them less. It's not a personal thing, but before they seemed to always hover over us. Now, the more we assume accountability, the more they delegate to us. They make sure we're pointed in the right direction, on the priorities of our clients, and other than that, they let us run."

"Bill, I believe the word is empowerment, something, frankly many departments, including mine, struggle with."

"I've rediscovered my passion. I actually enjoy being here. I more clearly see how I contribute value to my clients. By managing their expectations, things have really improved. We're on the same page."

"Wow! I guess I never thought about it that way," added Bob, "It almost reminds me of my college days when we'd pull all-nighters studying for a test. While it was tough, I really enjoyed those times."

"Yeah, that's a good way to describe what I feel. I also compare it to my competitive sports days. Where we would practice endless hours, hit the weight room, and continually push each other to get better. We had a common goal – winning – and it seemed we all realized we couldn't achieve it alone. A real sense of community was present – an emotional connection."

"Bill, from my perspective it seems that establishing an emotional connection – in the case of sports, winning, in the case of work, generating value – seems to pull people together. In a way, sharing a higher purpose causes us, individually, to work a bit harder. Simply put, its peer pressure, but in a positive sense."

"Work should give substance, meaning, and value to our lives. It should make us feel that we are contributing to the world, that we are somehow leaving a legacy ... help us focus not on ourselves but others, the beneficiaries of our work. It widens our horizons and connects us with others – with our teammates, with our organization, with our customers."

– Michael Hammer, Author
Beyond Re-Engineering

9
What's In It For Me?

In 2007, Towers Perrin shared the findings of a global study regarding employee engagement. They found that twenty-one percent of workers worldwide are engaged; whereas thirty-eight percent are either disengaged or disenchanted. Interestingly, as an outgrowth of this study, they didn't define employee engagement as satisfaction or happiness, but rather the degree to which workers connected to the company emotionally; the degree to which employees *were aware of what they needed to do to add value* and were willing to take action. Once again, by revisiting the earlier teeter-totter graphic, this conclusion seems to reinforce the need to add weight to side B.

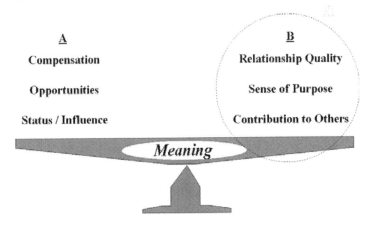

By structurally aligning individual agendas and work practices with organizational priorities, priorities that are focused on delivering value to others, successful organizations continually add weight to side B. This will result in a more engaged workforce and, in turn, a more productive, innovative, resilient and responsive organization. Yet, questions still remain. What's in it for *me* – beyond compensation, job security and/or career advancement? Why should I care? How will these value-based changes directly affect me, address my needs, my self-interests? Good questions; ones that BEST leaders are able to answer.

Less is More

Suffice to say, most people have good intentions. They go to work with the desire to work hard and get along with others. While there will always be exceptions, most people are good people. They want to contribute and use their time constructively. Yet, with that said, many people are over-worked or possibly, under-utilized.

They are unable to keep up, not necessarily due to lack of commitment, but instead, as the graphic suggests, due to lack of focus and prioritization … knowing *what* work to do. What activities are important, which ones aren't? The inability to answer this question leads to poor performance, frustration, cynicism, apathy, stress, and in turn, a host of health related consequences.

While establishing shared purpose and streamlining systems and services improve productivity and economic performance, they also directly improve individual effectiveness and happiness.

By building upon the earlier graphic, establishing shared purpose (the star) and streamlining systems and services (determining what work is necessary to achieve the star) provide the clear direction and focus that people require.

Activities that lie on the path can be accelerated, activities that lie outside the path eliminated, and activities partially on the path can be optimized. Teamwork – given this clear and shared direction – will improve, as will creativity, productivity, responsiveness, client satisfaction and employee health and morale.

Fueling the Tank

People require energy to make it through the day. Energy is reflected via one's creativity, passion, joy, hope and activism or involvement. People with positive energy brighten up the world around them. They see possibilities where others see obstacles – optimistic versus pessimistic. They love life, others and themselves.

For purposes here, these "sources" of energy can be broken into six forms – material, physical, intellectual, emotional, spiritual and social. The first three, for many people, are near capacity. Materially, people can only afford so much, and the positive effects of acquiring something new are fleeting or possibly even addicting; physically, while exercise and nutrition should be a priority, the positive effects by themselves fall short of achieving a greater sense of inner-joy or fuel. Intellectually, it is challenge to keep up with the pace of change. It's stimulating to learn new things, yet it seems many people are consumed by everyday demands. Additional energy or fuel is available via these aforementioned categories; however, it's limited. Yet, the remaining three categories – emotional, spiritual and social, are virtually limitless.

Emotional Energy...Relationship Quality: Today, many organizations are struggling with the effects of a fractured workplace. Relationships, internally and externally, have become less loyal and more transactional – for example, moving from conversation toward email. Emphasis has gradually shifted away from maximizing value to maximizing profits, and from interdependence and collective good toward independence and self-sufficiency.

Most people do not need to look too far to see the deterioration of relationships, whether in their personal or professional lives. It is so common that many people accept it as normal. People are increasingly challenged with the social pressures and dynamics found at work. Conflicting agendas, challenging personalities, excessive demands and lack of focus drain the energy from today's workforce, insidiously eroding performance and morale. In order to deliver sustainable results, organizational leaders must step up and address this escalating crisis of employee apathy and disengagement. Employees require an intrinsic source of motivation, a sense of meaning, purpose and contribution from their work. Without it, employees tend to rely on extrinsic (e.g., compensation, status, and advancement) sources of motivation, which cost more to administer and the motivational impact is short lived.

Spiritual Energy...Sense of Purpose: Religious choices and/or one's conception of a higher power are best left up to each individual. However, employees in developed societies, with their economic needs largely met, seek an increased sense of purpose or self-actualization with the knowledge that they are making a difference in the lives of others. Compensation, to a point, influences job satisfaction; however, studies have shown it does not ensure an engaged, productive and creative employee.

Historically, social dysfunction was a result of individual interests overshadowing the collective good or shared interests of others. By *structurally* aligning individual agendas and work practices with organizational priorities that are focused on delivering value to others, a greater sense of shared and/or higher purpose will result. This then allows people to reconcile differences, discover creative possibilities, and respect diverse contributions within the higher or broader context of how each party contributes to creating and delivering value to a particular set of customers and/or internal clients. In addition to improving the bottom line, this will result in a more unified sense of community by focusing attention on how people individually and collectively contribute to improving the lives of others.

Social Energy...Sense of Community: Humans are social creatures. We enjoy interacting with others, being part of extended communities or social networks. We extract energy and fulfillment by being part of a team, whether it is sports, garden club, civic initiative or organization, church group, et cetera. We build relationships, we grow, we learn, we challenge, but most importantly, we share a common purpose. Work, by creating a stronger sense of shared purpose, can fuel our need for social connection. Organizations recognize this inherent need. Many have 'open door' policies, encourage teamwork, celebrate events, accomplishments and holidays, and send gifts and flowers on special occasions. This helps people socially 'connect' with their company and their colleagues; however, the motivational effects are often short-lived. As organizations emphasize value, and show how people individually and collectively contribute to delivering it, a dynamic sense of shared purpose will result – a stronger sense of community. People will become more inspired and more connected, to each other and to the organization. They will enjoy their work and value their colleagues, and quite likely, work harder. Similar to off-season conditioning, required of sports, employees will be more inclined to invest in their physical and mental health during off-hours. Their attitudes regarding their employer will positively permeate their business relationships, families and community, retaining current employees and attracting future ones.

Dealing with Variation

In order to repeatedly deliver value to others, people and organizations need to improve how they work together internally and externally. People must become skilled at embracing diverse or opposing perspectives, reconciling differences, managing interdependencies and finding common ground. Unfortunately, many people find it easier to surround themselves with people who share similar beliefs or views. In the process, they attempt to avoid the inherent friction or risk that comes from associating with people of differing beliefs or views. In our personal life we are free to determine who we associate with, however, at work that is typically not the case. To be successful in today's interconnected world, people have to gain comfort reconciling differences and embracing viewpoints that run counter to their own. In many cases, they have to reconfigure regionalized or local practices that previously appealed to a particular department, organization or community. The shared beliefs that previously appealed to a particular group of people may now be preventing them from embracing others of dissimilar beliefs.

Today, due to technology advances that have eased the dissemination and access to information, speed is of the essence. Innovation or value creation, from conception to implementation, is continually accelerating. In many cases, technology advances have converted what previously took years into months and what took months into minutes. Therefore, while one head may be able to envision new ideas, two or three heads working together can do it a lot faster. Simply bringing smart and capable people in the same room does not ensure innovation or value will be created; often, it is just the opposite. Without a co-creative or synergistic approach and the willingness of individuals to follow it, progress and creativity may be impeded. People, in this scenario, become more concerned with defending their ideas and views. They listen, yet with the primary intent of positioning and interjecting *their* views. In a synergistic process, solutions are co-created, simultaneously morphing the ideas and contributions of multiple parties. In this context, listening focuses on building upon one another's views and contributions ("yes, and ...") versus only attempting to interject yours ("yes, but ...").

Although dealing with variation or conflict is challenging, it is also necessary. Individuals and organizations grow and evolve by being pushed and challenged, not by running in place. Similar to sports, *competitive* teams want to play tough competition in order to test their abilities and expose their weaknesses, enabling them to become stronger. The same can be said for business – variation and conflict cannot be avoided nor, in many respects, should it be.

Self Awareness

Many people, during their formative years, have experienced either the pain of non-acceptance or the thrill of victory, both of which frame their worldview and approach to dealing with conflict. Flight, fight or acquiesce? All of which are non-productive in today's increasingly turbulent work climate. To most people, these emotive triggers lay deep within their unconscious. People react based on life experiences, but in many cases, if asked, they are not sure why. They are not "aware" of certain unconscious triggers, pro and con, that lie deep within their persona.

Poor self-awareness limits one's ability to develop healthy and productive relationships with others. It is virtually impossible to manage expectations or find common ground with others when you, or your department, are not sure what you believe or why you believe it. By having better clarity on *what* and *why*, individuals will be in a far better position to work with others on *how*; blending strengths and compensating for weaknesses and blind spots.

Dr. Carl Jung, a prominent psychologist in the early 1900s, studied the unconscious side of human behavior. He believed, as few others did at the time, that all people have an unconscious side to their personality. Failure to understand this unconscious side results in various forms of personal dysfunction or difficulty, which significantly influences a person's behavior, attitude and ultimately their sense of happiness. Dr. Jung's work continues to influence modern approaches to psychotherapy, encouraging individuals to develop greater inner-consciousness or self-awareness in order to more effectively deal with outside challenges and/or difficult relationships.

In his national bestseller, *Emotional Intelligence*, author Daniel Goleman outlines four stages of emotional intelligence; each stage acts as a precursor to the next – self-awareness, self-management, social awareness and relationship management. Value-based change, like it or not, will disrupt current reality; it will alter previously held mindsets and worldviews. As a result, relationships will change. Using Mr. Goleman's emotional scale, in order to successfully reshape these relationships (i.e., stage 4) people must first be comfortable in their own skin, which is the first three stages: self-awareness, self-management and social awareness.

Self-awareness: In order to more effectively deal with opposition, difficult relationships or changing circumstances, people must learn to turn inward – assessing their response, right or wrong, to challenging situations. Are they able to constructively embrace differences or opposition? Do they fight it? Run from it? Hide or ignore it? In today's turbulent world, rather than reacting in historical and/or patterned ways, people must use challenging circumstances – which work provides – to become more introspective. They need to continually ask themselves, "Why does this situation or person bother me?" In many cases, the particular situation or person will not change nor go away; however, *how* a person reacts can change significantly. And, as a result, people will become increasingly more effective in dealing with variation or difference – an important trait in today's world. Relationships will become stronger, and interestingly, people will attain higher levels of inner-peace and happiness. Not because the situation necessarily changed, but instead because they changed how they personally dealt with it. While it may sound rather masochistic, learning to constructively deal with challenging or unexpected circumstances is an important means for personal growth. Difficult situations or relationships act as a mirror into one's inner-psyche. If allowed, they can surface historic, often hidden, mindsets and beliefs that are typically a result of life experiences or surroundings. These historic and hidden attitudes may be limiting one's day-to-day effectiveness, triggering bouts of anxiety or depression, and quite often are the source of emotional outbursts and/or withdrawal. Addictions, in various forms, temporarily fill inner-voids and/or allow people to ignore their inner-pain. Real healing will occur by making what's hidden, visible. Once visible, people can more effectively determine whether these historic traits help or hinder their interpersonal success in today's ever-changing and diverse world. While a person may decide not to change, they will at least have a better understanding of their decision and the potential consequences.

Self-management: When people increase their self-awareness, they find themselves in a better position to refine historic beliefs and assumptions, or at least mitigate the damage they may be causing. This stage is called self-management. Changing historic beliefs is extremely difficult. They are yours. They define you. They have shaped how you see yourself, possibly even determine who you opt to associate with. It's human nature that most people prefer to associate with people who share similar beliefs. These like-minded relationships tend to validate people, make them feel secure, and to a degree, in control of their lives. For example, one's attitude toward competitive situations may be largely responsible for life's successes and/or possibly life's failures. Some people may welcome competitive situations – they enjoy the battle; the mental, physical and emotional challenges that ensue. It both invigorates and motivates them. The point is their competitive attitudes are neither right nor wrong; they define who they are and how they tend to operate in certain situations. Problems, however, arise when belief-systems clash. For example, people approach competitive situations differently, yet, given their unique perspective and life experiences, equally effectively. In this example, if these people lack sufficient self-awareness (i.e., conscious grasp of their competitive instincts) or lack self-management skills (i.e., the ability and willingness to tailor their beliefs or approach based on situational or personality differences), social and/or relationship dysfunction is likely to result.

Social awareness: As people become increasingly more self-aware and develop self-management skills, they will be more equipped to effectively deal in a variety of social situations; they will be in touch with themselves and correspondingly more in touch with the needs of others. They will be better equipped to reconcile differences, find common ground and constructively co-create novel solutions by respecting the diverse, even opposing views of multiple parties, parties that may not share the same belief systems and more than likely do not look, think or act the same. In today's interconnected and changing world this is fast becoming the norm versus the exception.

Relationship management: Finally we arrive back at the fourth stage of Mr. Goleman's emotional scale – relationship management. In today's world everyone must be capable of strengthening current relationships and skilled at establishing new ones. Relationships, previously predicated on like beliefs, will now be a result of respecting, even welcoming unlike beliefs and worldviews. Problems are increasingly more complex and therefore new solutions – hence, new relationships – are necessary to address them. Previous competitors are becoming partners, suppliers are becoming customers, and today's enemies are becoming tomorrow's allies. Regional or provincial attitudes and mindsets – which will require collective self-awareness to redefine and/or rectify – may have served and protected historic interests in the past; however, they may be the very same attitudes that are preventing progress and social harmony in the future. While it's important for people, or communities for that matter, to have local interests and needs that must be considered, even protected, they must also recognize we are operating in a global, interconnected economy. We have technology advances and consumer demand to thank for this, but the fact is we now live in a multi-cultural world. Therefore, if behooves everyone to develop the self-awareness, self-management, social awareness and relationship management skills to succeed, or possibly even survive.

Picking up where their conversation left off ...

 "Bill, I must admit, I used to underestimate the importance of some of the policies we have around here. I saw them as bureaucratic and time consuming. Now my attitude has changed."

"I agree Bob. I never appreciated how these policies and procedures, done right, help minimize relationship problems and frankly make us more effective and productive."

"Sounds like you're ready for a management position," laughed Bob, realizing he was also considering increased job responsibilities.

"I think I am. I'm encouraged by what our organization has done recently. Before, as you know, we tended to look at our management in a rather negative way; however, now we're seeing them in a far more collaborative light. They are less forceful, and they're delegating more and more responsibility to us."

"That's great to hear. You'd make a great leader, you've taught me a lot over the past couple of months."

"Thanks Bob, but as I've said previously, I'm not real sure what we actually did or, if asked to do it again, how I'd even begin. Our discussions have been mutually enlightening. I've learned a lot too. My quandary, given our departments success to date, is that I may be asked to join another department to replicate what we did. I'm not sure I'm ready."

"Bill, from my perspective, you're ready. Once you get started, you'll do just fine."

God grant me the serenity

to accept the things I cannot change;

courage to change the things I can;

and wisdom to know the difference.

– Reinhold Niebuhr
The Serenity Prayer

10
Getting Started

To this point, this book provided a holistic look at the importance of creating a meaningful, productive and value-oriented workplace – focusing on *why* and *what*, which, in a manner of speaking, reflects one side of the coin. However, in order to secure support and move forward, you must also be in a position to address the other side of the coin – *how*. *How* can you mitigate risk? *How* can you engage your organization? *How* can you improve your odds of success? *How* can you do it affordably? Every situation, every organization, is different; therefore, so is the approach and priorities. Recognizing this, it would be difficult to be too prescriptive; what follows are suggestions on how to get started.

Crawl – Walk – Run

Let's first face facts, people don't like change. Also, managers are often reluctant or protective when asked to alter historic practices; practices that have fueled their power. This is reality. Group-think and/or historic norms tend to prevail; thus the reason most organizations struggle with successfully implementing change. Therefore, before you decide to plunge in, it is best to test the water; piloting concepts before expanding and institutionalizing them.

Pilot: Concepts presented in this book are not complex. The intent was to establish a common understanding, a voice. This will improve the ability to rally diverse viewpoints and ideologies around a common process. The pilot stage is used to convert these concepts into practice. The approach is two-fold.

115

One, where possible, identify existing examples and/or leaders who exemplify the BEST principles conveyed throughout this book. In most cases, they exist. However, their efforts may have been natural *to them*, instinctive, therefore, not always easy to put into words. Don't expect them to easily articulate their experiences. It's up to you to extract and discover how they established a sense of shared purpose within their team and how they streamlined systems and services in order to maximize the value they delivered. Look specifically in terms of new benefits, cost/waste reduction, time savings, resource utilization, improved margins, et cetera. Show how their efforts improved profitability, productivity, innovation, and customer service and employee morale. In this way, internal change champions will surface (most importantly, sharing a common language) and external concepts will be converted into internal stories – stories that people can better relate with.

Two, identify a prioritized area, a place to start – a market segment, customer, project or work unit. Establish measurable outcomes, targets, by using historical data (e.g., profit margins, cycle time, waste, return on innovation, productivity, employee and customer satisfaction), and attempt to utilize leaders that inherently exhibit BEST traits. The intent will be for them to first establish a shared vision. Keep in mind that a *vision* may take minutes to establish, whereas a *shared vision* may take months. This step alone will clarify assumptions and align agendas, identify priorities and goals, and increase workforce commitment. After clarifying their shared vision, leaders will then be in a position to streamline the systems and services necessary to achieve it – identifying their targeted customers and/or internal clients and their highest priorities and needs. This will allow them to optimize or eliminate low-value activity and incorporate new, higher-valued activities ... activities

116

necessary to achieve the shared vision. These two activities – establishing shared purpose and streamlining systems and services – significantly improve performance and result in a work environment that will build trust and accountability, and better tap talent.

Expand: Assuming a successful pilot stage (months, not days), leaders will now be in a better, more informed position to expand the principles deeper within their organization. For smaller and/or more centralized organizations, the pilot stage may be all that is required. In this case, the value-based principles are understood and can be institutionalized (see below). However, this is often not the case. In most situations, additional examples will need to be established, assessing different variables or situations, which in turn further mitigates risk on the part of leaders, and further engages the organization. These efforts will identify additional change champions and proactively surface potential obstacles in the form of policies, work processes, skill gaps and leadership traits.

Institutionalize: Eventually value-based concepts will need to become institutionalized – woven into the organization's culture. In large part, the Pilot and Engage stages were testing concepts and principles, in many cases, sailing against the wind of existing work practices, reward systems, power structures and/or beliefs. For example, hiring practices may change. How you train, reward and promote people will change. Leaders will now be judged less on their technical knowledge or positional power and more on their ability to streamline systems and services, their ability to maximize value and tap talent. As organizations pursue value-based changes, work practices and measures will change, as will policies and procedures. Interpersonal and leadership skills will need to be developed, and new relationships will need to be formed in and outside the organization. The point is change will happen!

In support of the above, GTP Associates (www.gtpassociates.com) can help organizations introduce value-based concepts in an affordable, practical and sustainable manner.

Managing the Journey

Regardless of which stage you're in – Pilot, Expand or Institutionalize – it will entail managing change, moving from what-is to what-is-desired. Therefore, it is important to follow some form of a roadmap or change process. This will allow you to better communicate, engage others, mobilize leaders, manage expectations, track progress and most importantly, significantly improve your odds of success.

Managing change is not as linear or clean as the following model depicts, but this three-step framework introduces a degree of order to a frequently misunderstood science – the ability to modify human behavior.

There is an extensive amount of material, books and training available on the subject of managing change, the intent here is to simply scratch the surface.

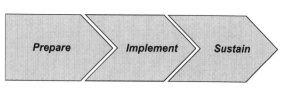

Prepare	Implement	Sustain
• Envision the Change	• Prioritize & Focus	• Measure & Communicate
• Secure Sponsorship	• Engage Others	• Reward & Celebrate
• Identify Champions	• Utilize Sponsors	• Refine & Expand
• Assess Readiness	• Manage Effort & Expectations	

Prepare

<u>Envision the Change</u>: At the risk of over-simplification, envision the end-in-mind. Remember the immediate goal is to

improve performance in terms of profit, growth and innovation (yet, in a manner that simultaneously improves workplace quality and effectiveness). So it's important to first get a reality check. What are leaders losing sleep over? Why? Talk to your boss, your boss's boss. Survey others, ask tough questions. What will a more meaningful and value-based environment yield? How will it make your organization better? How will it improve performance, address your existing priorities? How will it improve morale, make the workplace more creative, cooperative and productive? While many of these questions were addressed throughout this book, the answers were far from complete. Previous chapters simply painted the picture with rather broad strokes. The purpose here is for you to revisit these same questions, but in a manner that fits *your* situation, addresses *your* issues, *your* priorities.

Secure Sponsorship: Pioneering change requires agility and tact, the ability to read and react to changing winds. To succeed, or better yet survive, pioneers need to mobilize other leaders – secure sponsors, those individuals with influence and budget. Securing sponsorship has less to do with the brilliance of the idea and more to do with how the value-based changes align with the organization's strategies; thus the focus of earlier chapters and the previous step. While a key element to creating a value-based work environment is defining *what* it entails, emphasis should also be directed at *how* it's implemented in order to successfully mobilize the support of necessary leaders. Many changes fail because the pioneers pursuing them fall in the trap of idealism, overlooking the fact that the leaders they need to mobilize tend to be grounded in realism. In order to secure sponsorship, change pioneers must identify the intersection between what is necessary and what is feasible, aligning concepts, breadth and pace with situational reality and readiness.

Identify Champions: Take the time to identify and rally fellow ambassadors – people who are credible within their peer group and willing to champion the cause. In virtually any organization, people exist who see similar problems and if asked, would be willing to get involved. A word of caution, identifying champions may be the easy part, whereas rallying them around a common cause is a lot more challenging. Each of these potential champions may have different viewpoints, priorities and challenges. Or possibly, they share similar views, however, have a different way of articulating them. Some prodding and facilitation may be required to bring potential champions on board. You will need to help them see how a value-based workplace will address *their* issues, *their* concerns, and *their* self-interests.

Assess Readiness: Quite often, organizations struggle with implementing 'best practices' that were proven elsewhere. The concepts – in this case, improving value – are the same, yet their success at implementing them is radically different. As a result, a lot of money is wasted and leadership credibility is lost. Every situation is different, therefore so is the approach. For example, in one situation the morale and trust levels are high. People work well together, constructively share ideas and have a clear understanding of their different roles. In this example, due to their inherent readiness, they may be able to pursue more, do it faster, and have far greater odds of success. However, if this situation were reversed, and trust and cooperation was low, it would be wise to walk before you run, taking small steps in order to build credibility, trust, and ultimately, momentum. There are a multitude of considerations. Are current leaders autocratic or facilitative, skilled at leading change? Are there consistent work processes and metrics in place? Are sponsors skilled and willing to fulfill their role, do they have trust and credibility within the organization? What are potential obstacles? Dependencies? Do you have effective communication practices? Are people accountable? Are performance reviews in place? Is there an atmosphere of continual improvement? Service? Innovation? Cooperation? The point is every organization or situation is different and the more you are sensitized to contextual reality the better. In one situation, a fresh coat of paint is enough, whereas in another, the entire room may need to be rebuilt.

Implement

Prioritize and Focus: Few leaders have the time, patience or job security to invest in multi-year efforts before they begin to see signs of success. They want to see tangible results or they will quickly lose interest and/or alter priorities. In actual fact, that mentality is healthy. While creating a value-based work climate is a journey, establishing measurable and realistic milestones along the way is imperative. *Envisioning the Change*, discussed earlier, will help you define the playing field – what's in, what's not; however, that step isn't intended to translate the change into bite size, time-driven pieces. You cannot pursue everything. It is now time to be selective.

Engage Others: Once you have a plan in place and the necessary sponsorship, it's time to assign accountability – who, what and when. This converts concepts and intentions into actions and timelines. Teams will need to be formed and leaders identified. A charter must be established that articulates the objectives and desired outcomes. Key milestones should be identified and roles and responsibilities defined, both for the team itself and others who are affected by the changes. Often, it's tempting to jump into the details and/or work prematurely, in large part naively believing you're fully empowered to act ... you're not. Avoid this trap. Your ability to engage others, utilize your sponsors, and manage the expectations of others will ultimately determine your success.

Utilize Sponsors: Sponsorship is critical. Unfortunately, many change leaders believe sponsorship is necessary to launch an effort not necessarily implement it. This view is a recipe for failure. While sponsors may not be immersed in the details of the effort, they are the ones responsible to remove organizational obstacles and/or adjust project expectations in order to better match reality. Sponsors must be kept informed, well before issues arise. They should know their roles and responsibilities, in particular with regards to a successful implementation. Many change efforts fail and as a result, many change leaders ultimately take the fall due to their inability to effectively utilize their sponsors. The difficulty here should not be underestimated. It is tough managing the efforts of those people that *you*, in many cases, report to.

Manage Effort and Expectations: Managing expectations would be easy if what was originally envisioned was entirely accurate, leaders were completely mobilized, and the organization was effectively engaged. But in most cases, that's not likely. Therefore, while an element of implementation is tracking progress and holding others accountable, a large part of managing the effort is being flexible. Not wishy-washy, but flexible. Learn to read between the lines, sense the situation. Maybe the time isn't right? Maybe you're trying to do too much? Maybe leaders are not fully on board? Maybe you were wrong? The point is, avoid intellectual or hierarchical arrogance. Remember you are managing a journey, which requires trust and strong relationships; therefore, use your head but trust your heart. Things change. Expect the unexpected and learn to adjust accordingly. Don't see mistakes, resistance or setbacks as a sign of failure – more likely they are a sign of progress. While it's important to remain convicted as to the merits of a value-based work climate, don't become inflexible or locked-down on previously agreed plans and timelines. Remain fluid and receptive to alternative views and changing conditions. Above all, don't take yourself too seriously and don't be surprised by surprises.

Sustain

Measure and Communicate: During implementation it's easy to get consumed by the details, working closely with those others who are directly involved in the effort. Yet with that said, it's equally important to keep your eyes on the horizon, assessing progress and ensuring key stakeholders – sponsors and employees – are in the communication loop. You can only improve what you can measure, therefore ensure you have a balanced scorecard, one that reflects four elements. First, financial or performance based metrics, such as improved margins, waste elimination, rate of return on new innovation, cycle times, growth, et cetera. Second, track the impact on your customers, markets or possibly internal clients. For example, track satisfaction levels, service level performance, growth, profitability, and degree of collaboration. Third, assess process improvements, how effectively work is being done. Track changes to work practices, what bottlenecks have been eliminated, how work has been streamlined, even eliminated. Look for cost savings, quality improvements, cycle time improvements, and the rate and degree of acceptance of new practices and/or technologies. Finally, the fourth element measures the impact on the people or workforce. Here, look at such things as adoption of new skills, employee satisfaction, teamwork, productivity and creativity. Today, many organizations are able to track employee health and wellness, in terms of health care costs and absenteeism; where possible, measure it. Keep in mind, when it comes to effective communication, right-brain recipients will intuitively assess softer indicators, such as laughter, creative debate, coworker support, increased accountability, and new ideas and suggestions; however, left-brain recipients will require data and facts, therefore, be prepared and be balanced.

Reward and Celebrate: Big changes are usually a series of small changes. Therefore, ensure you recognize progress for what it is – small steps. Implementing change is exhausting. Realizing this, it's important to consciously create opportunities to celebrate. Not just at the end of the effort, when results are in, but during the process itself, during the turbulent transitional times when stress and chaos is likely to be at its peak. To be successful at leading change, you want to openly acknowledge the pain and also share the glory; shine light on the accomplishments of others, celebrate progress – reward effort, especially if you want it to reoccur.

Refine and Expand: Managing change – modifying human behavior – is difficult, even ugly. What may have been proven elsewhere, even within your own organization, is not necessarily replicable. It's tempting, for expediency sake, to simply package up prior learning's and deploy them elsewhere in your organization. To a degree, you can; however, you need to remain sensitive to the needs and priorities of those you will ultimately affect. This takes time, and more importantly, patience. A tendency, once we've experienced a small degree of internal success, is to 'package and push' concepts elsewhere within the organization; rushing past the preparation step, immediately into implementation. This approach may *appear* more expedient, but longer-term this approach rarely works. Why? This failure is not necessarily due to what's being asked, but instead it's due to the impersonal approach that was taken – failure to connect concepts with their situation, their reality.

In support of the above, GTP Associates (www.gtpassociates.com) can help catalyze change, teaching others to fish by providing a *voice*, *methodology* and *support* to internal change champions.

Our Time, Our Place

"The dogmas of the quiet past are inadequate to the stormy present. The occasion is piled high with difficulty, and we must rise with the occasion. As our case is new, so we must think anew and act anew."

– Abraham Lincoln

It's fair to say many of us are experiencing a "stormy present ... piled high with difficulty." Therefore, in the words of Abraham Lincoln, "we must rise to the occasion ... we must think anew and act anew." It's *our time* and it must occur in *our place* ... where many people spend the majority of their time – at work.

A couple months later ... Friday 5:30 p.m. ... as Bill and Bob were leaving work.

"Bob, what are your plans for the weekend?"

"Well Bill, tomorrow morning my daughter's soccer team is playing in the semi-finals of our league playoffs. Myself, and the other coaches, are hosting a cookout this evening with the kids and their parents, pump a little motivational juices into them for tomorrow's game."

"Win or lose time, eh?" asked Bill.

"Not exactly. Actually we never discuss winning or losing, but only playing our best, learning and supporting one another. This attitude has permeated both our players and, equally important, their parents.

Sound familiar? I'm only applying what I've learned here at work. In many respects, I've applied a value-based attitude to coaching this team. Everybody now trusts that their fellow players will be in position when they pass the ball and vice versa. Winning now seems to be more of an end result, not necessarily the goal. Like here at work, the kids are far more unified and they actually enjoy the hard work that goes into getting better. Our success has attracted a number of compliments from opposing coaches; in one case, a fellow coach even inquired as to how we have achieved it. It reminded me of how we began our discussions a few months ago."

"Bob, I'm amazed. Not only has your work life taken a turn for the better, I'm seeing the old Bob reemerge. Your energy and enthusiasm is contagious!"

"Bill, I can't thank you enough. I didn't realize how my work life was so intertwined with my personal life. I always believed I did a good job of managing them separately. My job, however, was slowly draining the life out of me, and I didn't even realize how significant it was. These last few months have reenergized me!"

"That's great, I'm happy for you."

"Bill, what is most ironic is that my happiness is not due to spending less time in the office. I'll actually be spending a few hours here over the weekend, but a big difference now is the fact that I want to! I guess it is another counter-intuitive benefit we can discuss at another time."

"Character cannot be developed in ease and quiet. Only through experience of trial and suffering can the soul be strengthened, ambition inspired, and success achieved."

– Helen Keller

About the Author

I am both an optimist and a realist, a practitioner not a theorist. I have lived that which I believe. During my twenty-plus years with Dow Corning Corporation (their turnaround story was shared in earlier chapters), I experienced how the quality of the workplace simultaneously influences both organizational performance and personal fulfillment. I experienced the lows – dysfunctional relationships, conflicting agendas and poor leadership – and was fortunate enough to play a role in creating new highs. Seeing the positive results in terms of bottom-line performance, customer service, relationship quality, employee engagement and leadership effectiveness was exhilarating. A more meaningful and productive workplace ensued, and I'm proud to have been a part of that cultural transformation. It was quite a ride.

In 2002, with their new value-centered strategy successfully launched, I left Dow Corning, with their blessings, in order to reflect upon my experiences and share them with others. I created GTP Associates – **G**rowth **T**hrough **P**eople – in order to assist others in Bringing Meaning into Monday, providing sustainable and practical ways to succeed in their professional, personal and spiritual lives.

I encourage you to use this book as a basic guide for your future success. It is intended to shine light on the importance of *how* you conduct business by reawakening a timeless and universal truth – those who serve, prosper. Or, as my kids might say, the more you give the more you get.

If you would like further information or additional support please visit www.gtpassociates.com.

"We are not human beings having a spiritual experience. We are spiritual beings having a human experience."

– Teilhard de Chardin

Acknowledgments

I want to first thank my former colleagues at Dow Corning Corporation (Midland, MI). I had the privilege of working around the world, learning from various cultures and the people that represented them. These relationships showed me that there are universal ideals shared by all, which I've attempted to reflect in this book. There is a special place in my heart for those fellow change agents that helped transform the company during rather turbulent times – individuals willing to sail against the wind. There were hundreds; however, while in my commercial capacity, I worked closely with a handful – Mary Lou, Laura, Eriko, Jamie, Sean, Rebecca, Randy, Endvar, Jack, Ed, Chris, Ian, Marjorie, Melanie and Siegfried. In addition, two people, Tom Cook and Philippe Rovere, stood out. Tom, who in our formative IT years helped refine and validate my views, and later, in our commercial roles was instrumental in putting them into practice. Philippe, whose drive helped birth the value-based principles shared in this book and whose humility allowed them to be successfully implemented.

While at Dow Corning, the profit-based side of the coin was defined, however, it was necessary for me to leave in order to fully define the other side of the coin, the people-based side. That desire has brought other people into my life that helped mold my views. Jon Kabbe, whose eclectic wisdom and perspectives helped broaden and deepen mine. Tim Adams, your business savvy is helpful, but witnessing your personal transformation was inspirational. Bob Plewa, you helped me see the unseen; in particular, the role energy plays in our lives, in our health, in our happiness. Pastor Tony Waldrop, for trusting a foreigner with your congregation, allowing

131

me to pilot a program entitled *Healing the Hurt* – in hindsight, the teacher was the pupil. Deb Cull; thanks for your "film crew" support and your willingness to help me wade through earlier versions of this manuscript; Stephanie Damore thank you for guiding me through the final stages of editing and publication; and thanks to Mark Bush for your contributions to cover design.

Finally, I want to acknowledge the support of my family. First my extended family, you've all played a part in shaping my views over the years. Mom, this book is dedicated to you because you've role-modeled the importance of faith and family, and the value of perseverance. Tim, being the elder sibling, you paved the way. I've been fortunate to learn from your mistakes ... and yes, your insights. Jeff, who like me, tends to draw outside the lines ... the picture is finally coming together, we'll title it *The Road to Ashland*. Mary Kay (born with cerebral palsy), having you in my life has allowed me to experience the world from a different angle. To my kids, Alysia and Drew, you both helped me realize the importance of building a better world, and the role leaders (and parents) play in achieving it. And finally to my wife and friend, Cyndi, thanks. Wherever our lives lead, I'm a better person for having you in mine.

Made in the USA